Essential Histories

The Anglo-Irish War

The Troubles of 1913–1922

Peter Cottrell

Essential Histories

The Anglo-Irish War

The Troubles of 1913–1922

First published in Great Britain in 2006 by Osprey Publishing,
Midland House, West Way, Botley, Oxford OX2 0PH, UK
443 Park Avenue South, New York, NY 10016, USA
E-mail: info@ospreypublishing.com

ISBN 1 84603 023 4

Series Editor: Professor Robert O'Neill
Design: Ken Vail Graphic Design, Cambridge, UK
Index by Alan Thatcher
Maps by The Map Studio
Originated by PPS Grasmere, Leeds, UK
Printed and bound in China through Bookbuilders

06 07 08 09 10   10 9 8 7 6 5 4 3 2 1

A CIP catalogue record for this book is available from the British
Library

FOR A CATALOGUE OF ALL BOOKS PUBLISHED BY OSPREY
MILITARY AND AVIATION PLEASE CONTACT:

NORTH AMERICA
Osprey Direct, c/o Random House Distribution Center,
400 Hahn Road, Westminster, MD 21157
E-mail: info@ospreydirect.com

ALL OTHER REGIONS
Osprey Direct UK, P.O. Box 140 Wellingborough, Northants,
NN8 2FA, UK
E-mail: info@ospreydirect.co.uk

www.ospreypublishing.com

Dedication
In memory of my grandfather, 82476 Sgt William Leonard
Cottrell of the 9th Bn The Cheshire Regt, who was based at the
Curragh, Co. Kildare in the spring of 1918.

Acknowledgements
I would like to thank Richard Abbott, Jim Herlihy, Kevin Myers,
Keith Strange and my wife Heather for all their help and support.

Contents

Introduction

It is likely that many people have never heard of the Anglo-Irish War. Many of those who have probably know very little about it, other than that it is one of the many messy conflicts that serve as footnotes to the First World War of 1914–18. Some have probably heard of the 'Black and Tans', and doubtless have come across stories of the controversial Michael Collins, subject of many books and a major feature film. Most will be familiar with the Irish Republican Army (IRA), Sinn Féin, Orangemen and the Ulster Volunteer Force (UVF) because of 35 years of sectarian violence in Northern Ireland. Less well known is the fact that none of these organizations emerged in the 1960s, but instead had their roots in a time when Ireland was part of the United Kingdom.

Although the Anglo-Irish War, or the 'War of Independence' or 'the Troubles', as it has variously been called, receives little attention in Britain, it is remembered in Ireland through the perpetuation of an 'official' Nationalist 'Liberation myth'. This myth made Nationalist icons of Eamon de Valera, Michael Collins and others whilst vilifying the British as perfidious colonial oppressors to such an extent that this version of history has largely been allowed to go unchallenged. Consequently, it is extremely difficult to discern what is myth and what is fact regarding the events that took place in Ireland and Britain between 1913 and 1923. Unfortunately, some versions of Irish history have been so tainted with half-truths and fabrications that at times it is almost impossible to discern fact from fiction.

In his book *The Black and Tans* Richard Bennett labelled the Anglo-Irish conflict as one that 'the English have struggled to forget and the Irish cannot help but remember'. Yet what is it exactly that the British have struggled to forget and why is it that the Irish cannot help but remember? Arguably the British have no desire to remember a conflict that in their eyes saw the secession of what had been for 121 years an integral part of the United Kingdom, whilst the Irish remember British brutality. Just as many US perceptions of the American Revolution are distorted by their own foundation myth, Irish Nationalist histories tend to throw up stereotypical caricatures of the British as monsters driven by anti-Irish xenophobia. This version of events tends to ignore the fact that both sides committed atrocities.

It also ignores a significant fact about British rule in Ireland: that it would have been impossible without the support of thousands of Irishmen, in the army, the police and the Civil Service; or, indeed, without the acquiescence of the vast majority of the population of Ireland. Although the history of British Ireland is littered with rebellions, nearly all of them were put down by both British and Irish troops. The rebels may have labelled these Irishmen as 'traitors' but in the words of Sean O'Faolain, who was both in the IRA and the son of a policeman during the conflict, 'Men like my father were dragged out … and shot down as traitors to their country … they were not traitors. They had their loyalties, and stuck to them.'

Despite the contentious issues of Unionist and Nationalist politics that dogged pre-First World War Ireland, over 200,000 Irishmen volunteered to fight for 'King and Country' in the war. Some, like Tom Barry and Emmett Dalton, returned to join the IRA and became violent revolutionaries, whilst others drifted into the ranks of the Royal Irish Constabulary (RIC). In that respect the Anglo-Irish War was as much a civil war as an 'international' conflict, and as such did not end with British withdrawal in 1922 but

POLICE NOTICE

£1000 REWARD.

WANTED FOR MURDER IN IRELAND

DANIEL BREEN

(calls himself Commandant of the Third Tipperary Brigade).

Age 27, 5 feet 7 inches in height, bronzed complexion, dark hair (long in front), grey eyes, short cocked nose, stout build, weight about 12 stone, clean shaven ; sulky bulldog appearance ; looks rather like a blacksmith coming from work ; wears cap pulled well down over face.

The above reward will be paid by the Irish Authorities, to any person not in the Public Service who may give information resulting in his arrest.

Information to be given at any Police Station.

Although the RIC offered substantial rewards for the capture of IRA activists, few were captured as a result of wanted posters like this one. (Courtesy of the RUC George Cross Foundation)

with the end of the 'official' civil war in 1923, and arguably not even then. Equally, it is sometimes difficult to establish when the Anglo-Irish War actually began. Traditionally it is seen as beginning when Dan Breen and members of the Tipperary IRA ambushed and killed two Irish Catholic policemen – Constables James McDonnell and Patrick O'Connell – in a quarry near Soloheadbeg, Co. Tipperary on 21 January 1919. This is because this was the first of many incidents when the IRA deliberately targeted policemen. Some analysts see the Easter Rising in 1916 as the start of the war, whilst others place its roots even earlier in Anglo-Irish history.

Republican interpretations tend to see every rebellion from the Anglo-Norman invasion of 1169 to the present day as part of a continuous struggle for liberation from English, or British, rule. However, this is far too simplistic an interpretation of Anglo-Irish relations, since the Catholic rebels of the 1640s recognized Charles I's right to be King of Ireland, as did the Irish Army that fought for James II. Only the predominantly Protestant-led United Irishmen fought for a non-sectarian Republic along Franco-American lines. Republicanism was not the central thread of Nationalist resistance to British domination of Ireland, and even Sinn Féin was a constitutional monarchist party when it was founded in 1905.

Although Ireland's many insurrections were not part of a continuous struggle for liberation, it would equally be wrong to say that earlier rebellions did not inspire or affect those that came after them. If Republicanism was not a significant feature of Irish rebellions before 1798, it was to become the dominant feature of 19th-century Irish subversion. Despite financial and moral support from Irish émigrés in the US, none of the Republican efforts before 1921 were successful in freeing Ireland from

British rule. In fact, from the failure of the Fenian Rising in 1867 to the period immediately before the First World War, Ireland was a relatively peaceful and prosperous part of the UK. However it was by no means united, and despite the high-minded non-sectarian ideals of the United Irishmen, Ireland was a deeply divided society. Sectarian violence bubbled beneath the surface and political allegiances were often dictated by sectarian tribal loyalties. In the non-conformist Protestant heartland of Ulster most of the residents feared any form of devolved or independent Dublin-based government, because they would become a minority in a Catholic-dominated independent Ireland, which re-awoke folk memories of the massacres of Protestants during the 1640s and the 1798 rebellion.

In response to the rising tide of constitutional Nationalism, with its goal of a devolved Irish government in Dublin, the Protestant North began to mobilize against the possibility of Irish Home Rule. The year 1913 saw the creation of pro- and anti-Home Rule paramilitary groups, firstly in the guise of the Ulster Volunteer Force (UVF) and then in response the National Volunteers; both promptly began to smuggle arms into the country. The battle lines of some form of Irish 'civil war' were being drawn in 1913, and although hostilities were temporarily postponed in August 1914 when the UK declared war on Germany, it was only a stay of execution that lasted until 1919.

The compromise treaty that ended the conflict and partitioned Ireland turned out to be the catalyst for the civil war that bitterly divided southern Irish society, and created the political parties that still define the Republic's politics. Within living memory, veterans of these events dominated Irish politics and it is hardly surprising that they cast a shadow over Anglo-Irish diplomatic relations and bequeathed a bitter legacy to both the Royal Ulster Constabulary (RUC) and the *Garda Síochána* (Garda).

Ultimately, it is only since the deaths of the likes of Eamon de Valera, who took part

Provinces of Ireland

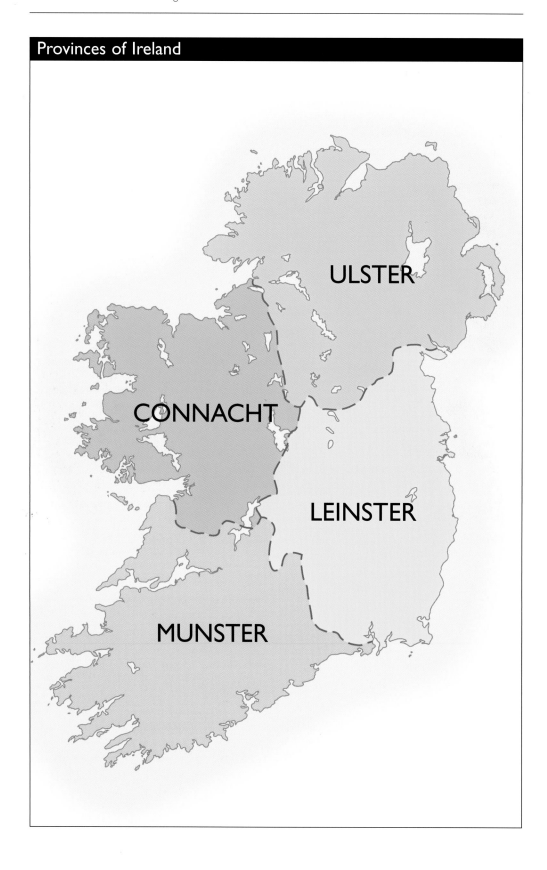

in the struggle, that Irish historians have begun to question traditional Nationalist interpretations and come to terms with their past as a piece of historical study rather than an emotional experience. Despite this revisionist renaissance, very little has been written about the conflict in the United Kingdom outside of Ulster or the realms of academia, and the British public remain largely ignorant of the conflict that shaped modern Ireland and its relationship with Britain.

Officers of the North Down 1st Battalion UVF. There were strong links between religion and politics amongst the Ulster Paramilitaries. (Courtesy of the Ulster Museum)

Chronology

1169 Anglo-Norman invasion of Ireland.

1172 The Pope recognizes Henry II of England as *'Overlord'* of Ireland.

1690 **1 July** William of Orange defeats the Irish Army of James II at the battle of the Boyne, and ensures the Protestant Ascendancy.

1795 Orange Order founded.

1798 United Irishmen revolt fails. The rebellion degenerates into a series of sectarian massacres by both rebel and government forces and is ruthlessly suppressed by British and Protestant-led Catholic Irish troops.

1801 Act of Union. Ireland becomes an integral part of the United Kingdom. The Irish Parliament in Dublin dissolves itself and Irish MPs become members of the Westminster Parliament.

1867 **6 September** The Fenian revolt, the last serious 19th-century attempt to overthrow Britain, fails. The Irish Constabulary is awarded the title 'Royal' for their part in suppressing the rebellion.

1905 **28 November** Sinn Féin League founded by Arthur Griffith, an Irish journalist of Welsh extraction.

1912 **11 April** Third Home Rule Bill introduced to Parliament.

1913 **13 January** Sir Edward Carson founds the Ulster Volunteer Force (UVF) to oppose Home Rule by force if necessary.
31 August Riots in Dublin give Ireland her first Bloody Sunday when the Dublin Metropolitan Police disperse crowds in Sackville (now O'Connell) Street, Dublin.
25 November The National Volunteers are established as a response to the creation of the UVF.

1914 **March** The Curragh 'Mutiny' – British Army officers in Ireland threaten to resign if they are ordered to suppress Unionist opposition to Irish Home Rule. The 'mutiny' created a crisis in Ireland that was only diffused by the outbreak of the First World War.
25 April The police do nothing to prevent the UVF landing 24,600 German rifles at Larne and Bangor, Co. Down.
26 July The police and army attempt to prevent pro-Home Rule National Volunteers from landing 1,500 rifles at Howth, Co. Dublin, and troops shoot three civilians during a disturbance in Dublin.
4 August Britain declares war on Germany.
8 August The Defence of the Realm Act (DORA) passed, giving the police and army emergency powers in the entire United Kingdom, not just Ireland.
24 September Anti-war members of the National Volunteers split to form the Irish Volunteers under Eoin MacNeill.

1916 **24 April–1 May** The Easter Rising (Dublin).

1917 **25 September** Thomas Ashe, leading Irish Republican Brotherhood (IRB) and Sinn Féin activist, dies whilst on hunger strike in British custody.

1918 **August** Unofficially the Irish Volunteers are increasingly referred to as the IRA although this title was not formally adopted until 1919.
11 November Armistice ends fighting on the Western Front.

14 December Sinn Féin wins a landslide victory in the General Election, which it takes as a mandate to declare 'independence' from the UK.

1919   **21 January** Dáil Éireann meets in Dublin. The IRA ambushes and kills two Royal Irish Constabulary (RIC) constables at Soloheadbeg, Co. Tipperary: the traditional start date of the Anglo-Irish War.
31 January Piaras Beaslai incites the IRA to target the RIC in an article in the Volunteers newspaper *An tÓglach*.
8 September The 'sack' of Fermoy.

1920   **25 March** RIC recruits from mainland Britain begin to arrive in Ireland. Due to kit shortages they are issued with a mixture of police and army clothing. Their appearance gives rise to the nickname the 'Black and Tans'.
4 June The IRA orders a boycott of the RIC and their families.
27 July First recruits join the Auxiliary Division RIC (ADRIC).
9 August Restoration of Order in Ireland Act (ROIA) passed.
26 August Ulster Special Constabulary (USC) formed.
20 September The 'sack' of Balbriggan.
21 November The IRA assassinates 12 men believed to be British intelligence officers; at least one was not an intelligence officer. Later the same day, 14 civilians are shot dead by policemen in Croke Park, Dublin, giving the world Ireland's second Bloody Sunday.
28 November IRA ambushes and kills 17 RIC Auxiliaries at Kilmichael, Co. Cork.
23 December The Government of Ireland Act (sometimes known as Fourth Home Rule Bill) is passed. Under the act Lloyd George proposed the division of Ireland into a self-governing Southern and Northern Ireland, still answerable to the British Government on issues relating to the Crown, defence, foreign affairs, international trade and currency.

1921   **25 May** The IRA attacks and burns down the Customs House in Dublin.
11 July Anglo-Irish Truce.
6 December Anglo-Irish Treaty signed. This effectively confirmed the partition of Ireland enshrined in the 1920 Government of Ireland Act. Both sides accept a compromise that involves the partition of Ireland and the retention of the monarchy in Southern Ireland.

1922   **16 January** The Lord Lieutenant of Ireland, Edward Talbot Fitzalan, hands Dublin Castle to Michael Collins and the provisional Government of Ireland takes over the government of Saorstát Éireann (Irish Free State) as a Dominion within the Empire, with King George V as head of state.
21 February Civic Guards formed in the Irish Free-State.
13 April Anti-Treaty IRA under Rory O'Connor occupies the Four Courts in Dublin.
31 May RIC disbanded.
1 June RUC formed.
28 June Irish 'civil war' breaks out between pro- and anti-Treaty factions of the IRA when Tom Ennis leads pro-Treaty troops against the rebels occupying the Four Courts.
22 August Michael Collins killed in an IRA ambush.

1923   **24 May** Irish 'civil war' ends when the IRA Chief of Staff Liam Lynch is killed and the remaining IRA 'Irregulars' are told to dump arms and go home.
8 August Civic Guards re-named the *Garda Síochána*.

A troubled island

Some believe that the Anglo-Irish War has its roots in the Norman invasion of 1169, which resulted in the kings of England becoming the titular rulers of Ireland. Although there may be some merit in this argument it is too much of a sweeping generalization. In reality, the conflict of 1913–22 had its roots in the failures of the 1798 United Irishmen rebellion, in constitutional Nationalism, the agrarian disasters of the 1840s and the rise of militant Hiberno-American Republicanism.

Anglo-Norman and later Anglo-Scots colonists undoubtedly enmeshed Ireland in mainland British politics, but it did not take long for them to become 'hiberniores hibernis ipsos' (more Irish than the Irish), much as the Danes and Gaels had done before them. So long as the country's nobility paid lip-service to the King's Writ they were left more or less to their own devices, whilst the Crown only tended to pay attention when there was a threat to its authority or when foreign invasion loomed. In the final analysis it was not the Normans that fragmented Irish society and sowed the seeds for the sectarian divisions that have plagued modern Irish history – that dubious honour goes to the Reformation. The Protestant Reformation and the Catholic Counter-Reformation of the 16th and 17th centuries not only divided Ireland, but also plunged Europe into a cultural civil war that intertwined religion and politics to the extent that non-conformity to the State religion, whatever it might be, was tantamount to treason.

In 1541, Henry VIII of England had himself declared King of Ireland in Dublin. He was determined to break the power of both the Anglo-Irish barons and the Gaelic-Irish chieftains, and began a process of strengthening Ireland's central government that his successors happily continued. A feature of this was the confiscation of rebel lands and its redistribution to settlers who established plantations. These new planters were inevitably Protestant, although the system was developed under the Catholic Queen Mary and proved to be the template for the future colonization of Protestant North America. Whilst many of Ireland's Anglo-Irish lords embraced Protestantism, others remained faithful to the old religion. Unfortunately this made scores of them, along with their Scots and English co-religionists, susceptible to exploitation by Catholic France and Spain. In an age when, to many Scots, Englishmen and even some Irishmen, Catholicism not only represented theological degeneracy but also disloyalty to the Crown, it was relatively easy for English-speaking Britons, whether they be Scots, Irish, Welsh or English, to view the Catholic Gaelic-Irish as an alien, dangerous and subversive influence. Ultimately, the Reformation and the plantations created a socio-economic underclass of the Gaelic-Irish Catholic majority who were governed and looked down on by an Anglo-Irish Protestant minority.

Ironically, in a reversal of modern perspectives of Ireland, Dublin was the centre of British influence whilst Ulster was the centre of resistance to Ireland's central government. In 1607 the rebel earls of Tyrone and Tyrconnell went into exile and the British sought to fill the resultant vacuum through plantations. Most of the planters in north-eastern Ireland were Scots Presbyterians, and thus as Dissenters excluded from power, but still the process of transforming Ulster into the Crown's most loyal, if not peaceful province, had begun.

In 1641, dispossessed Ulster Catholics rose up to reclaim their property. This rebellion was the final spark that lit the fuse that culminated in the English Civil War. These Irish rebels

Plantations of Ireland

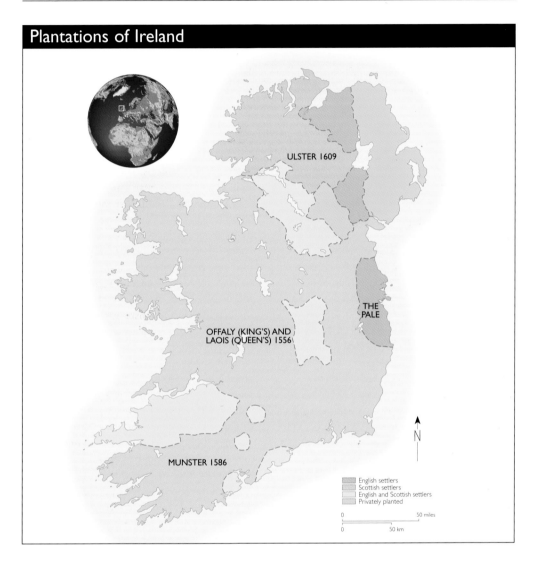

ULSTER 1609

THE PALE

OFFALY (KING'S) AND LAOIS (QUEEN'S) 1556

MUNSTER 1586

N

English settlers
Scottish settlers
English and Scottish settlers
Privately planted

0   50 miles
0   50 km

never disputed the English king Charles I's right to be King of Ireland, unlike his English Parliamentarian enemies who defeated, deposed and executed him. Much has been written of Cromwell's ruthless suppression of the Catholic Confederacy to the extent that he has entered Irish mythology as a xenophobic bogeyman. This view usually ignores the British context of his campaign where Cromwell ruthlessly suppressed any resistance – English, Scottish, Irish or Welsh – to his new Commonwealth. Ultimately, the destruction of the English Royalist garrison of Drogheda, and of Royalist privateers in Wexford, pales into insignificance next to the excesses of the Thirty Years' War.

Before 1798, none of the rebellions were about breaking the link between the Irish and English Crowns; in fact, between 1689 and 1691 thousands of Irishmen fought to restore James II to his English throne. It is true that the Williamite victories on the Boyne and Aughrim, still celebrated by Northern Irish Unionists to this day, may have guaranteed Protestant Ascendancy even if this campaign was only a minor sideshow in a larger European war. For a hundred years after these victories, anti-Catholic Penal Laws discriminated against the Catholic majority; however, their repeal in 1778–82 allowed Catholic families to be listed once more amongst landowning classes.

A distinctive feature of rural Irish society was the proliferation of 'secret' societies that, under cover of darkness, imposed their own version of social justice. The punishment beatings by Catholic Defenders or Whiteboys and Protestant Peep O'Day Boys were as much about economic grievances as sectarian ones. The United Irishmen rebellion of 1798 may well have been intended as a Jacobin secular revolt, but because of ingrained sectarianism in many areas it degenerated into massacre and counter-massacre by Catholic and Protestant mobs.

The rebellion of 1798 had not begun as an excuse for discontent Catholic peasants to massacre their Protestant landlords and run amok; its inspiration was the secular French Revolution that destroyed the Ancien Régime in 1789. Its leaders sought to create a non-sectarian Irish Republic of Protestants, Catholics and Dissenters as United Irishmen, breaking the link between Ireland and England. Revolutionary France, which had been at war with England since 1793, was more than happy to supply arms and troops to attack her vulnerable Irish flank. Unfortunately, the revolt was badly organized, poorly led and French help arrived too late to make any difference. Although 'The '98' as it became known was consigned by government troops to the pantheon of heroic failures that pepper Irish history, it remains significant for one reason – it was the symbolic birth of the Irish Republican Movement.

The net result was that an Act of Union removed Ireland's legal independence in 1801 and the Irish Government became an administrative department of the British Government, headed initially by the Lord Lieutenant but later by his Chief Secretary. Its location in Dublin Castle gave it its nickname – the Castle. It was apparent that opposition to the Crown was the one thing that prevented political change in Ireland, as an independent Irish Republic was utterly unacceptable to the British. Despite economic decline and famine during the early 19th century and the failure of Irish MPs to break the Union, the lot of Ireland's Catholics steadily improved. Catholic emancipation and hard-won land reform ensured that Irish Catholics began to share in the country's prosperity, and by 1921 over 400,000 of the country's 470,000 smallholdings were owned by Catholic occupiers.

Although abortive rebellions continued, 19th-century mainstream Nationalism followed constitutional lines with the Irish Parliamentary Party (IPP) MPs disrupting and frustrating Parliament's business to publicize Irish issues. The IPP, formed in 1882, originated from the Home Government Association, which favoured limited self-government for Ireland; it became powerful under Charles Parnell in the latter part of the 19th century. Home Rule and Land Reform became the twin threads of their agenda, and despite several failures they finally got a Home Rule Bill passed in 1914. Home Rule fell far short of the Ireland envisaged by the United Irishmen, and only conceded a limited form of devolved government, similar to that in Scotland and Wales today. Of course, not everyone in Ireland was content with Home Rule, and Protestants in north-east Ulster vehemently opposed it.

Once the heartland of Irish Republicanism, the Union had brought economic prosperity to Ulster. It was the only part of Ireland to benefit from the Industrial Revolution, and shipbuilding and linen turned Belfast into a major imperial city on a par with mainland cities like Glasgow. Concerns about Catholic-dominated, Dublin-based government and the perceived threat to their prosperity played on sectarian fears, and gave rise to a revival of secret Loyalist societies, defence associations and ultimately the creation of the paramilitary Ulster Volunteer Force (UVF) in 1913 to oppose Home Rule by force. To Ulster's Protestants, Home Rule was nothing less than Rome Rule.

Not surprisingly, most Britons viewed Ireland as an integral part of the UK even if they did not understand its politics – the majority of Britain's political parties, especially the Conservatives, supported Ireland's Unionists. It was a significant recruiting ground for the army, and a disproportionately high percentage of the

British Army's senior officers, from Wellington to Sir Henry Wilson, were Irishmen by birth, albeit Protestants. So much so that Protestant Irishmen, and especially Ulster Protestants, formed what Robin Neillands once referred to as the nearest thing to a *Junker* class that the British have ever known. Unsurprisingly this meant that Unionist sympathies were common amongst British Army officers.

Despite the steady improvements in Ireland's lot, 'physical force' Nationalism did not end with the failures of 1798, and secret Republican societies endured. Invariably they failed, through bad planning or betrayal by ubiquitous police informers; however, they did produce a steady crop of martyrs, heroic failures and stirring patriotic ballads. In addition, appalling land management practices combined with famines killed or displaced millions of people willing to believe in the Nationalist folk-myth of some idyllic pre-British past. Significantly the waves of emigration that these events caused created large Irish communities outside of the UK with bitter memories of the British.

The most significant Irish émigrés, both then and now, were those who crossed the Atlantic to Britain's first lost colony, the USA. Many Irish-Americans hoped for the day when they could return and throw off the 'yoke of Saxon tyranny' that, in their eyes, was responsible for all of Ireland's ills. So it was that in 1858 and 1859 two revolutionary secret societies, the Irish Republican Brotherhood (IRB) and the Fenian Brotherhood were formed. In 1866 the Fenians unsuccessfully raided Canada and ultimately their only significance was that the rebels called themselves the 'Irish Republican Army' or IRA for the first time. Their aspirations came to naught in 1867 when yet another poorly organized coup failed to liberate Ireland.

The Irish diaspora in Australia also retained an interest in the events unfolding in the 'old country'. Dr Daniel Mannix, an Irishman by birth, an old friend of De Valera and the Catholic Archbishop of Melbourne, spoke in support of Irish Independence in New York in July 1920. When he attempted to visit Ireland in August 1920 a British warship intercepted his ship and prevented him from setting foot in the country. In December 1920 another Australian, the Archbishop of Perth, acted as an intermediary between the Irish Under Secretary, Sir John Anderson and Arthur Griffiths. For a brief moment it looked like peace negotiations would begin until the British Prime Minister, Lloyd George, insisted that no rapprochement could be made with the rebels until the IRA surrendered its arms.

The Fenians did not intend to fight pitched battles with the army, and so 1798 was the last time that these took place. In fact, subsequent insurrections tended to be dealt with by the police, and as a reward for their efforts in frustrating the 1867 uprising the Irish Constabulary became the Royal Irish Constabulary. This shift in emphasis subtly changed the would-be rebel from a soldier fighting for his nation into a common criminal. After 1867, the IRB began to play a more significant role, and after a period of stasis it began to infiltrate the spectrum of Nationalist organizations, the Civil Service and even the police.

By 1913 Ireland may have appeared a relatively stable and prosperous province of the United Kingdom; however, beneath the surface it was a troubled island riddled with sectarian and political divisions. The pro- and anti-Home Rule factions threatened civil war through the UVF and National Volunteers, whilst the issue was made worse by several senior army officers who threatened to resign if they were ordered to suppress Unionist opposition to Home Rule. To compound the issue, the Irish Socialist Republican Party (ISRP) formed its own militia, the Irish Citizen Army (ICA), raising in the eyes of the Castle fears of some sort of Bolshevik uprising. It would seem that as long as every Irish political party had its own paramilitary organization, any form of political change was faced with the threat of violence. Meanwhile, the IRB continued their systematic infiltration of Nationalist societies and cultural organizations, biding their time. Ultimately the Home Rule crisis was overshadowed by the outbreak of war in 1914. In the end it proved to be nothing more than a stay of execution.

The combatants

The Crown forces

The seat of British administration in Ireland was Dublin Castle ('the Castle'), where the Chief Secretary headed an Irish civil administration renowned for its incompetence and inefficiency. Unlike Wales or Scotland, however, Ireland had a Lord Lieutenant or Viceroy to represent the monarch. The Crown relied upon both the police and the army to enforce the rule of law and, despite efforts to show otherwise, the vast majority of civil servants, policemen and soldiers who made British rule possible were Irish Catholics.

In 1914 over 22,000 Irishmen were in the Regular Army, with 33,000 listed as reservists, and by 1918 over 200,000 had fought for King and Country. Ireland was divided into three military districts: Northern (Belfast), Midland (Curragh) and Southern (Cork), whilst Dublin was a separate sub-district, and between 1914 and 1918 thousands of men were trained there. By November 1919 there were 34 infantry battalions stationed in Ireland undergoing a process of demobilization, training and reorganization. Six battalions were disbanded, and the old districts were reorganized into the 5th Division, commanded by MajGen Sir Hugh Jeudwine based in the Curragh, and the 6th Division, under MajGen Sir Peter Strickland based in Cork. Dublin remained an independent command. By July 1921 over

A British Army patrol on the streets of an Irish town, 1920. (Courtesy of National Library of Ireland, Photographic Archive)

50,000 troops were scattered across Ireland to support the police. It is worth noting that in August 1920 14 infantry battalions (about 14,000 men) fulfilled the same role in mainland Britain.

With the exception of the fighting during Easter Week 1916, the army conducted few conventional military operations during the Troubles. Only 25 per cent of Ireland was ever under martial law and most of its activities were centred on Dublin and Munster. Unsurprisingly, its officers tended to be rather conservative and harboured Unionist sympathies.

The army that emerged from the First World War was in many ways different from the one that had marched off in 1914. It was war-weary, battle-hardened and utterly

The Badge of the RIC. (Courtesy of the RUC George Cross Foundation)

STATION BADGES, ROYAL IRISH CONSTABULARY.

unprepared for the coming conflict. Many soldiers could not take the Troubles seriously, whilst others were prepared to apply solutions more appropriate to a trench-raid rather than to a civil emergency within the UK. The relationship between the army and police was never clear, and despite martial law in some areas the military tended to play second fiddle to the civil authorities.

As the Crown's representatives in the community, the police bore the brunt of Republican violence between 1918 and 1922. Out of approximately 17,000 or so Irish police, 513 were killed and 682 wounded whilst their friends and families were intimidated and ostracized. There were two constabularies in Ireland: the Royal Irish Constabulary (RIC) and the Dublin Metropolitan Police (DMP). The 1,202-strong DMP was responsible for the greater Dublin area and its members were indistinguishable from their mainland colleagues. Although most of the senior officers were Protestants, some, like Assistant Commissioner Quinn, were Catholics. The DMP relied on the

18 armed, plain-clothes detectives of G Division, a cross between the CID and Special Branch, to monitor political dissidents and investigate ordinary crimes. Charged with policing a population of 304,000 Dubliners it had an unsatisfactory working relationship with both the RIC Special Branch and the Secret Service. Neither organization trusted it because of its poor track record, and by 1921 the IRA had murdered six so-called G-Men. Of course, unbeknown to either organization, its failings were mainly because four of its detectives were active members of the IRA.

Despite accusations that the RIC was a foreign gendarmerie imposing colonial rule, the overwhelming majority of policemen were Irish. About 70 per cent of the other ranks were Catholics whilst 60 per cent of the officers were Protestant, and in 1913 they were seen as a legitimate force even if their involvement in evictions did nothing for

DMP senior officers in full dress uniform and DMP constables in Dublin Castle. (Courtesy of National Library of Ireland, Photographic Archive)

their popularity. Despite their stations being called barracks they were in reality ordinary houses, rather than military installations, accommodating up to half-a-dozen men, and resembled rural police houses elsewhere in the UK. The most controversial elements of the RIC were the Temporary Constables and the Temporary Cadets of the ADRIC (or 'Auxies'). Because of kit shortages the Temporary Constables were forced to wear a mixture of RIC green and army khaki uniforms, and soon they were nicknamed Black and Tans after a famous pack of hunting hounds. Despite their folk-myth image, the Tans were never a separate organization but short-service policemen who served alongside the Regular RIC. What made them stand out was that many of them were not Irish (although a significant number of them were). Incidentally, the British public did not view the 26 per cent of mainland British policemen who had been born in Ireland as foreigners.

The Auxies are often confused with the Tans and erroneously treated as the same. They were not. The ADRIC were mostly ex-officers recruited specifically to form anti-IRA companies that would operate independently of the rest of the RIC. Irish folk-myth remembers the Tans as brutal foreigners recruited from English gaols, but in reality the 2,200 men of the ADRIC held 632 gallantry awards; Cadets George Onions and James Leach had won the VC; Cadet Bernard Beard MC had been a Brigadier General; and many were Irish by birth. It is easy to forget the long shadow that the First World War cast over the young men who joined the RIC, or even the IRA, after coming of age in the

RIC Auxiliaries in Cork 1921. (Courtesy of National Library of Ireland, Photographic Archive)

Police casualties

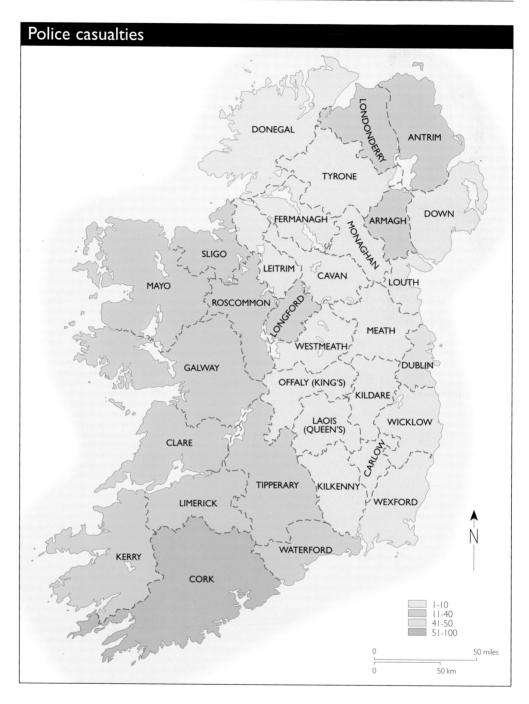

trenches. Disillusioned and brutalized, they brought a degree of ruthlessness to the conflict that was probably unthinkable before 1914.

Another controversial police force was the Ulster Special Constabulary (USC), raised on 26 August 1920. The USC was independent from the RIC and organized into a full-time

element called the 'A Specials' and two part-time groups – the 'B' and 'C Specials'. What made the USC radically different from the RIC, DMP or even the army was that it was essentially raised from one of Ireland's paramilitary groups – the Ulster Volunteer Force (UVF). Although they were both Irish

A British propaganda postcard showing the RIC, Black and Tans and ADRIC all working in harmony against the IRA. (Courtesy of Jim Herlihy)

Gallantry awards held by the ADRIC	
Award	*Number*
Victoria Cross	2
Conspicuous Gallantry Medal	2
Distinguished Service Order	22
Military Cross	130
Distinguished Conduct Medal	23
Military Medal	63
Foreign Awards	40
Order of Merit	1
Mentioned In Despatches	350
Total:	633

Protestants, Field Marshal Sir Henry Wilson (Chief of the Imperial General Staff) and General Sir Nevil Macready (General Officer Commanding in Chief – Ireland) had reservations about using the UVF as policemen, and controversy surrounded the USC until it was disbanded in 1970.

The Loyalists

The Ulster Unionist Council (UUC), founded in March 1905 in conjunction with the Orange Order, was at the forefront of Unionist resistance to the prospect of Protestants becoming a minority in a Catholic-dominated 'independent' Ireland. On 13 January 1913, Sir Edward Carson and Sir James Craig founded the UVF to resist Irish Home Rule by force if necessary. Both the army and the Government tolerated the UVF and, despite its overt threat to plunge the country into civil war, it was allowed to smuggle weapons into Ulster and to drill openly under the instruction of both retired and serving army officers.

During the First World War the UVF formed the 36th (Ulster) Division and suffered heavy casualties on the Somme. Even though it was not the only region to suffer in the war, many Ulstermen believed that this loss was a 'blood tax' that had placed Britain in their debt. The upsurge in IRA violence revitalized the post-war UVF

F.M. Sir Henry Wilson was a staunch Unionist who had reservations about using the UVF as Special Constables. (Courtesy of Hulton Archive/Getty Images)

and it was in an attempt to keep them under control that the Government formed the USC. The 'B Specials' later earned a place in Republican folk-myth that had previously been reserved for the Black and Tans, and they are still the subject of much debate today.

The Nationalists

By 1913, Nationalist Ireland encompassed both constitutional reformers and subversive revolutionaries. John Redmond was the leader of the Irish Parliamentary Party (IPP) and the man responsible for getting the third Home Rule Bill introduced to Parliament in 1912. Tragically for constitutional Nationalists he was unable to get the Act onto the Statute Book before the outbreak of war in 1914. On 25 November 1913,

Redmond gained control of the newly formed National Volunteers ('Volunteers') to counter the threat posed by the UVF. They never enjoyed the same level of government tolerance as the UVF, and when they landed weapons at Howth, Co. Dublin in July 1914, attempts were made to stop them. Involved in this incident was Erskine Childers, an unlikely revolutionary. Although born in Ireland he was of English stock. He fought for the British in the Boer War, worked as a clerk in the House of Commons for 15 years and

Sir Edward Carson inspects UVF volunteers in 1913. (Courtesy of National Library of Ireland, Photographic Archive)

was married to an American. He was a keen sailor who wrote *The Riddle of the Sands* and smuggled arms into Ireland in 1914 for the Volunteers. He was a passionate Republican and despite being the secretary to the rebel delegation that negotiated the Treaty he joined the irregulars during the civil war. Sneeringly known as the 'Englishman' behind his back he was executed by the Free State government in November 1922 for illegally owning a pistol. Ironically the weapon that cost him his life had been a gift

from his friend Michael Collins. The subsequent enquiry criticized the police's actions and the Deputy Commissioner of the DMP, William Harrell, was forced to resign.

Redmond encouraged his Volunteers to answer the call to arms in 1914, and despite some British resistance they formed the bulk of the 16th (Irish) Division. The Volunteers

ABOVE John Redmond presents new colours to Irish National Volunteers in 1913. (Courtesy of National Library of Ireland, Photographic Archive)

LEFT DMP Assistant Commissioner William Harrell. (Courtesy of Jim Herlihy)

were divided by the war and in September 1914 Eoin MacNeill led a splinter group called the Irish Volunteers. Unbeknown to its membership, this faction had been thoroughly infiltrated by the secretive Irish Republican Brotherhood (IRB), which had its own agenda. MacNeill disapproved of the 1916 Easter Rising, and countermanded the call to arms issued by Padraig Pearse. Unsurprisingly, the army defeated Pearse and his Dublin rebels.

Socialism, as well as Nationalism, was a potent force in pre-war Ireland and militant trade unionism gained a significant influence over its emerging urban working class in both Dublin and Belfast. The dock strike and Dublin lockout of 1913 were characterized by violent clashes between the police and

A joint Army–RIC patrol hunting for IRA Volunteers near Limerick. (Courtesy of National Library of Ireland, Photographic Archive)

strikers, and James Connolly, an Irish–Glaswegian ex-soldier, created the Irish Citizen Army (ICA) as a workers' defence force. The ICA, with its Marxist agenda, was never a large organization, and combined with Pearse's Volunteers to stage the Easter Rising. After the defeat of the Easter rebels the Volunteers and the IRB sat back, licked their wounds and reorganized for next time.

The British reaction to 1916 and the failure to achieve Home Rule undermined support for the IPP and increased that of Sinn Féin. Roughly translated as 'ourselves alone', Sinn Féin began life in 1905 as a pacifist Nationalist organization that favoured an Austro-Hungarian 'dual monarchy' solution to the Anglo-Irish question. Its founder, Arthur Griffith, was no pacifist but felt that violence was a spent force in Irish politics. Contrary to British opinion, Sinn Féin was not responsible for the Easter Rising. However, in its aftermath IRB men like Eamon de Valera and Michael Collins managed to informally link the Irish

Volunteers to Sinn Féin to effectively become its paramilitary arm – the IRA.

It is difficult to know exactly how large the IRA actually was. Its nominal strength of well over 70,000 all-ranks was organized along British Army lines linked to Sinn Féin and theoretically under the control of the rebel Dáil. The *Dáil Éireann* (Assembly of Ireland) was the extralegal 'parliament' formed by Sinn Fein MPs who refused to recognize the British Parliament. It first convened in Dublin at Mansion House in 1919 and soon after went underground. The reality was somewhat different and most played little or no significant part in the struggle – it is likely that there were fewer than 3,000 active guerrillas. This hardcore, bound by local loyalties and

Irish Citizen Army outside Liberty Hall. (Courtesy of National Library of Ireland, Photographic Archive)

often beyond effective control, were at the heart of IRA operations forming 'flying columns' of 20–100 men. Generally speaking, they distrusted ex-servicemen although some, like Emmett Dalton MC, Martin Doyle VC MM and Tom Barry, joined and were willing to act ruthlessly to prove their Republican credentials. Collins also created a team of gunmen, 'the Squad', for special duties who, along with his network of sympathetic G-Men, police, soldiers and even the Castle's classified cipher clerk, allowed him to wage a vicious war of terror and counter-terror against Britain's security apparatus.

By 'any means necessary'

By 1912, John Redmond, MP for New Ross, Co. Wexford, had convinced the Liberal Prime Minister Henry Herbert Asquith to introduce a Home Rule Bill to Parliament. Despite Asquith's reservations, the Liberals were dependent upon the Irish Parliamentary Party to form a government and had little alternative. Unionists vehemently opposed the Bill and Irish Republicans also had their objections. Unionists believed it was the thin end of the wedge, whilst Republicans felt it did not go far enough because it fell short of an independent republic. Ireland would remain an integral part of the UK with a devolved regional government, which was why Republicans objected to it.

Ulster Unionists signed a 'Solemn League and Covenant' on 28 September 1912, pledging to resist Home Rule, although many believed the threats were a bluff. In January 1913, Carson suggested the creation of a Protestant militia to back the Covenant's implicit threat of violence, and so the Ulster Volunteer Force (UVF) was born. Field Marshal Lord Roberts persuaded retired General Sir George Richardson to lead the UVF and he established an efficient HQ. Colonel Hacket Pain became his Chief of Staff, and it soon became obvious that the UVF was capable of preventing Home Rule in Ulster. The Government's lack of resolve prompted Redmond to create the National Volunteers in response.

In March 1914, General Sir Henry Paget, Commander in Chief in Ireland, was ordered to prepare for UVF violence. The Government gave Paget vague verbal instructions implying that officers from Ulster would be excused duty against the UVF whilst others could resign if they wished, effectively giving them the choice of which orders they would or would not obey.

Brigadier General Sir Hubert Gough and 57 officers from his Curragh-based Cavalry Brigade chose to resign if ordered against the UVF. Major General Sir Charles Ferguson's Curragh-based 5th Division refused to join the 'mutiny' but it was clear that the mutineers were not alone. The Government was losing control of the army in the face of the threat of a European war. The Chief of the Imperial General Staff, Sir John French, wrote to Gough assuring him that the army would not be used in Ulster. Home Rule was dead in the water.

War saved Ireland from its troubles and many Irishmen believed that Britain had gone to war to defend the rights of a small nation, Belgium, so logically Ireland's rights would be respected after the war. Although the war split the Volunteers, thousands of Irish Nationalists volunteered to fight for 'King and Country'. 200,000 Irishmen – Orange, Green and indifferent – signed up voluntarily. Although the Government allowed the UVF-dominated 36th Division to use 'Ulster' in their name, it objected to either the 10th and 16th Divisions using 'Irish' in theirs. All three divisions served with distinction, with the 10th suffering appalling casualties at Gallipoli and the 16th and 36th supporting each other on the Western Front.

By 1916 the Irish Republican Brotherhood (IRB) led by Padraig Pearse, Tom Clarke, Thomas MacDonagh, Eamonn Ceant and Eamon de Valera had gained control of what was left of the Volunteers. Amongst these hard-liners was an Anglo-Irish diplomat, Sir Roger Casement. In 1914 he was working to rally support for the revolution in the USA and Germany. His reception in the US was decidedly lukewarm and the Germans over-estimated Republican support in Ireland. Casement was genuinely surprised

Areas of disturbance

DONEGAL

LONDONDERRY

ANTRIM

TYRONE

FERMANAGH

MONAGHAN

ARMAGH

DOWN

SLIGO

LEITRIM

CAVAN

LOUTH

MAYO

ROSCOMMON

LONGFORD

MEATH

WESTMEATH

GALWAY

DUBLIN

OFFALY (KING'S)

KILDARE

LAOIS
(QUEEN'S)

WICKLOW

CLARE

CARLOW

TIPPERARY

KILKENNY

LIMERICK

WEXFORD

KERRY

WATERFORD

CORK

N

1907
1919
1920

0   50 miles

0   50 km

at the hostility of Irish prisoners of war when he attempted to raise an anti-British Irish Brigade in 1915. He only managed to recruit 55 men from over 2,000 Irish POWs. Worse still he realized that his recruits were unreliable self-seeking rogues. In the end, his plans came to naught and he became convinced that an Irish rising would be doomed to failure and resolved to return to Ireland to prevent one.

Arguably, Pearse did not care whether a rising succeeded or not, and there is considerable evidence to suggest that he had more enthusiasm for a heroic failure rather

The centre of Dublin was reduced to ruins during the fighting of 1916. (Courtesy of National Library of Ireland, Photographic Archive)

than success. Perhaps he realized that his brand of militant Republicanism, with all its martial imagery and rhetoric, was not actually that popular amongst the Irish and that his aims could only be achieved by provoking the British to over-react. It is equally possible that these hardcore revolutionaries were so divorced from reality that they felt that all they had to do was rise up and declare a Republic and every man in Ireland would rally around the green flag.

Either way, this minority within a minority was determined to rebel, and despite Eoin MacNeill's opposition they went ahead with their plans. Thus, on Easter Monday 1916, parties of Irish Volunteers and ICA seized strategic locations around Dublin and Pearse declared, 'in the name of dead generations', an Irish Republic from the main entrance of the General Post Office (GPO) on Sackville (now O'Connell) Street. The Easter Rising had begun.

British diplomat turned Irish rebel, Sir Roger Casement was executed for his part in the events of 1916. (Courtesy of National Library of Ireland, Photographic Archive)

The Easter Rising

It is probably a testimony to both the incompetence of the Castle and their perceived irrelevance of Pearse that the rebellion came as a surprise to both Government and the majority of Irishmen. The Royal Navy had cracked Germany's diplomatic codes early in 1915 and was well aware of Casement's movements in both the USA and Germany. One British official, Colonel Edgeworth-Johnstone, warned the Government that Sinn Féin was getting better organized and on 12 April 1916, the same day that a U-Boat left Germany carrying Casement, the Royal Irish Constabulary (RIC) was asked to examine the feasibility of arresting its leaders. Disturbingly, the RIC never replied to the Castle's request.

On 18 April, the news of Casement's departure had reached the British along with the news that the Germans were in the act of dispatching 20,000 rifles, ten machine guns and 5,000,000 rounds of ammunition to Ireland. The Royal Navy intercepted these arms on 22 April and Casement was arrested within hours of landing. Both events were kept quiet by the Castle although rumours of rebellion and German plots were rife. On the evening of 23 April, the Lord Lieutenant Lord Wimborne and the Chief Secretary Sir Matthew Nathan decided that in the circumstances they should arrest all of the leading Sinn Féin and Irish Volunteers leaders still at liberty. Ironically their decision came too late, as the rebels struck the next morning, on Easter Monday, 24 April 1916.

The Rising began in confusion for both the Castle and the Irish Volunteers. Monday was a Bank Holiday, and also Race Day at the Fairyhouse racetrack, so the streets were largely deserted when around 1,000 men of

The Four Courts, the centre of the Irish justice system, saw fighting in 1916 and again during the Irish Civil War. (Courtesy of National Library of Ireland, Photographic Archive)

the Irish Volunteers and ICA, under cover of a routine parade, seized some two dozen key points across the city. Pearse, calling himself the Commandant-General of the IRA, led the party that occupied the GPO in Sackville Street. Thomas MacDonagh seized the Jacobs Biscuit Factory behind Dublin Castle, but the rebels failed to take Trinity College when the University Officer Training Corps and some porters routed them after a brief tussle. Edward Daly took the Four Courts – the heart of Ireland's legal system – and some Volunteers and ICA dug in on St Stephen's Green, although rifle-fire from the Shelbourne Hotel later made them retreat into the Royal College of Surgeons. Eamonn Ceant took the South Dublin Workhouse and Eamon de Valera commanded the party that had seized Boland's flourmill.

Much to the bemusement of passers-by, Pearse, dressed in a Volunteer uniform crowned with a Boer-style slouch hat, stood on the front step of the Post Office and declared that Ireland was an independent republic, free from the oppression of the British. Most worryingly, the declaration highlighted the support of 'gallant allies in Europe' ignoring the fact that tens of thousands of Irishmen were fighting against those very allies in France and Belgium. Pearse had hoped that this call-to-arms would galvanize Irish resolve and that ordinary people would flock to their aid. Sadly for the rebels this expectation was based on very flawed and over-optimistic evidence. MacNeill, the Volunteers' Chief of Staff, was convinced that a rising would be unpopular and doomed to failure and withdrew his support. Over 100 Volunteers mobilized in Limerick but MacNeill told them to go home. Contradictory orders flew back and forth across the country and as a result many Volunteers simply stayed at home.

In Castlebellingham, Co. Louth, Volunteers under Sean MacEntee – who had failed to get a commission in the British Army only 12 months before – captured RIC Constable McGee and an officer from the Grenadier Guards and summarily shot them. McGee died of his wounds but the army

officer, left for dead, later recovered. Volunteers in Ulster attempted to rise in Belfast and Co. Tyrone but their efforts lacked cohesion and petered out. Enniscorthy was taken over by Volunteers on 27 April without a shot being fired, whilst its RIC contingent barricaded themselves inside their station.

Commandant Thomas Ashe ambushed 40 RIC men under the command of a District Inspector near Ashbourne, and after a five-hour firefight killed eight, wounded 15 and captured the remainder who surrendered when they ran out of ammunition. Ashe's ambush was probably the high point of the rebellion outside Dublin, whilst its low point was probably the surrender of 600 Volunteers on the historically significant Vinegar Hill after barely firing a shot. In the end, under 2,000 of the 13,000 or so known Volunteers attempted to do anything.

Meanwhile, in Dublin the main rebel enclaves were ignorant of what was happening across the country and despite his optimism Pearse had little grasp of the true situation. Their plan seemed to have been little more than to seize key points and await the British response. No one really knew what was going on, and the Irish poet James Stephens recalled in his journal of *The Insurrection in Dublin* that he had witnessed a workman being gunned down near St Stephen's Green when he attempted to extract his horse-drawn lorry from a rebel barricade. His impression was that ordinary Dubliners did not approve of what was taking place. Although the GPO had been taken without a shot, the killing had begun in the Upper Yard of Dublin Castle when rebels mortally wounded 48-year-old Dublin Metropolitan Police (DMP) Constable James O'Brien from Kilfergus, Co. Limerick, and occupied the yard. Capturing the Castle could have been a decisive coup for the IRA because the Chief Secretary was within its walls at the time. However, they failed to appreciate that the six soldiers they had captured were the only garrison, and inexplicably withdrew to some buildings opposite its gate. By early afternoon the

Castle was occupied by troops of the 3rd Battalion, The Royal Irish Rifles (RIR) and the 10th battalion, The Royal Dublin Fusiliers (RDF) and the moment was lost.

A party of IRA bluffed their way into the Magazine Fort on the pretence of recovering their football in order to destroy the ammunition stored there. The raid was frustrated because the Orderly Officer had taken the keys with him to the races. Ultimately, this attack did little to damage the British major arms dump, and resulted in the killing of the unarmed 17-year-old son of a British officer as he attempted to raise the alarm. Ironically, the first troops to react to the rebels were Irish, and within an hour of the shooting beginning most of the rebel enclaves were cordoned off by soldiers from two Irish regiments: 3 RIR and 10 RDF. Once contained, the rebels were subjected to a systematic bombardment by field guns and the gunboat HMS *Asgard*, anchored in the Liffey. The shelling did appalling damage to the centre of the city and went some way towards shifting public sympathy, if not support, from the army onto the rebels. The IRA may have gunned down several innocent bystanders, but they certainly did not hold the monopoly for illegal killings. The most controversial British killing happened on the evening of 25 April. Acting on his own initiative, a certain Captain Bowen-Colthurst of 3 RIR arrested and summarily executed a prominent Dublin journalist, Mr Sheehy Skeffington, and two others in the courtyard of Portobello Barracks. The Captain was later found to be mentally unstable, but although he had also shot an unarmed youth called Coade in Rathmines Street he was not dismissed from the army.

De Valera's men managed to give the Sherwood Foresters' Regiment a mauling near the junction of Northumberland Road and Mount Street Bridge, inflicting over 234 casualties, but by Saturday 29 April Pearse began to realize that his rebellion had failed. The centre of Dublin was in ruins, 16,000 British troops including six Irish battalions had the bulk of his forces bottled up in blazing ruined buildings, whilst 220 civilians had been killed in the crossfire and over 600 more were wounded. In six days of fighting, 134 British soldiers and policemen were dead and 381 wounded, whilst 64 rebels had also become casualties. Pearse no longer seemed keen on what he had once referred to as 'the red wine of battle', and at 3.30pm surrendered unconditionally to the British commander Brigadier General W.H.M. Lowe.

Pearse and his compatriots were guilty of treason in wartime and collaboration with the King's enemies, and as such had committed a capital crime. Considering Britain had been at war for two years and the rebels were, whether they liked it or not, British citizens, the Government's response was predictable if rather ill-advised. In accordance with the Defence of the Realm Act (DORA) the British were perfectly entitled to court-martial and execute them. This, after all, was the traditional fate of failed rebels everwhere. In all, military courts tried 160 of the rebels, and 15, including the signatories of the Declaration of Independence, were eventually executed. Even though the trials were perfectly legal under DORA, their relative secrecy and the lack of an appeal process increased sympathy for the rebels. Irish MPs protested against the executions and to make matters worse the Prime Minister seemed to have no control over the army.

There is no doubt that the British mishandled the aftermath of the Rising. However it is worth noting that 11 rebels were acquitted whilst 97 of those sentenced to death had their sentences commuted to life imprisonment. Amongst those so reprieved was De Valera, the only rebel leader to escape execution on the grounds that he was an American citizen. In addition 1,841 other rebels, including the future IRA leader Michael Collins, were interned in a detention camp at Frongoch in North Wales, although most were released between December 1916 and June 1917.

FOLLOWING PAGE The GPO and Nelson's pillar in the aftermath of the Easter Rising. (Courtesy of National Library of Ireland, Photographic Archive)

Irish prisoners being released from Kilmainham gaol, Dublin, by British soldiers during Nationalist unrest. (Photo by Central Press/Getty Images, © Central Press/Stringer)

The gathering storm

The IRA's command structure had effectively been decapitated by the failure of the Easter Rising, and the majority of militant Republicans found themselves behind bars in mainland Britain, but by June 1917 most of the Easter rebels had been released and were well placed to infiltrate Sinn Féin.

The Irish public did not rally to the rebels; in fact, many felt that Pearse and his cohorts had betrayed the Nationalist cause. DORA gave the army the authority to arrest, intern and try individuals without recourse to the civil judicial system. However, the army's activities simply infuriated innocent civilians, drove them into the arms of the Republicans and made them increasingly reluctant to come forward as witnesses.

This was good for Sinn Féin as it capitalized on the IPP's waning fortunes and began to portray itself as the only true Nationalist party. In common with other Nationalist organs after 1917, Sinn Féin was thoroughly infiltrated by militant Republicans and particularly the IRA. These personal links between the militant and political arms of Republicanism were so close that, although it was not responsible for orchestrating the 1916 rebellion, some British newspapers and officials began to refer to the 1916 Rising as the 'Sinn Féin Revolt' and its

De Valera on the election trail. (Courtesy of National Library of Ireland, Photographic Archive)

supporters as 'Shinners'. This perception was further reinforced when De Valera was elected President of Sinn Féin in 1917 and on 26 October called for Nationalist Ireland to unite against the British.

At the heart of Sinn Féin's strategy was the refusal to accept British rule and the creation of an underground Irish Republic acting as an alternative government that encouraged people to boycott British institutions. A spin-off of this policy was that the police, as local representatives of the British State, were increasingly being drawn into the conflict. In addition, the Government was increasingly conscious that the army's response to the Easter Rising had done more harm than good for their cause. The Government's public image was further dented when Republican prisoners refused to wear prison uniforms and those on hunger strike were force-fed. Things became even worse when Commandant Ashe of Ashbourne fame died after being force-fed on 25 September 1917, creating yet another rebel martyr.

The unpopular extension of conscription to Ireland in 1918 handed Sinn Féin an effective weapon to further undermine both the Castle and its police. Under a new generation of leaders like De Valera and Collins, Sinn Féin and the IRA used their time wisely to prepare for the struggle to come. Sinn Féin's appeal was also increased by the Government's ban on emigration and the extension of the franchise to all men over 21 and women over 30.

Ultimately, Sinn Féin managed to translate this support into overwhelming victory in the 1918 General Election on 14 December, by winning 73 out of 105 seats.

Sinn Féin candidates stood for election on the basis that they would not take their seats in Westminster but would convene an Irish Parliament, or *Dáil Éireann*, in Dublin, and felt that the election result was the mandate it required for rejecting British authority.

On 21 January 1919 the Dáil met in the Dublin Mansion House claiming to be the first Irish national political assembly to meet since the Irish Parliament was dissolved in 1801. Every Irish MP, whether Nationalist or

Unionist, was invited, although in reality only those 27 Sinn Féin MPs who were not in prison attended whilst the Unionists and IPP boycotted it and attended the Westminster Parliament. The official constitution of the Dáil was read out along with the offices of State, although the names of their incumbents were not made public until later.

When the Dáil reconvened on 1 April 1919, De Valera, who had escaped from Lincoln Gaol on 3 February, was appointed President of the Dáil and Prime Minister of Ireland. The 2nd Dáil also announced the names of the Republic's Officers of State: Arthur Griffith – Home Affairs; Count Plunkett – Foreign Affairs; Eoin MacNeill – Industry; Cathal Brugha – Defence; Constance Markievicz – Labour; William Cosgrave – Local Government; Michael Collins – Finance. All of them were either IRB or had had connections to it, as did Richard Mulcahy, a veteran of the Ashbourne ambush, who became Chief of Staff of the Volunteers, or IRA, in March 1918. Despite winning the majority of the Irish vote in 1918 Sinn Féin and the Dáil was unable to gain recognition from the Westminster Parliament as the legitimate government of Ireland. The simple fact was that neither party was willing or able to recognize the other's authority in Ireland. Redmond's support for the war damaged the IPP's support in Ireland. Their failure to win the Roscommon by-election in February 1917 signaled the beginning of the end and Redmond's death in March 1918 further hastened the decline of the party. The General Election in December 1918 saw the end of constitutional nationalism as the IPP's 83 seats in Westminster were slashed to just six. By 1921 the IPP had ceased to contest elections in the south.

Sinn Féin was not the only Nationalist/Republican organization to change its tack after the Rising – the IRA realized that the age of glorious gestures, meeting as one rebel song had it, 'by the rising of the moon' to fight pitched battles against the British Army, had passed forever. Consequently, 1916 was to be the last time that British troops and Irish rebels would fight each other in anything resembling large-scale conventional military operations. Ironically, the next time the IRA would meet government troops in the streets of Dublin would be the summer of 1922, and then the troops would be Irish.

Sinn Féin prisoners after being released in 1919. (Courtesy of National Library of Ireland, Photographic Archive)

Although fewer than 64 rebels had been killed or wounded during the Rising, and only 15 out of the 112 sentenced to death were actually executed, the British had effectively decapitated the IRA Volunteers' command structure. Redmond's death in March 1918 hastened the decline of the IPP whilst Sinn Féin's aggressive propaganda campaign combined with the British preoccupation with the First World War allowed a new generation of hard-liners to step forward into the vacuum that had been left. The new men – De Valera, Collins, Brugha, Mulcahy, Boland and their ilk – were veterans of 1916 who shared a ruthless determination to end British rule by any means necessary. On 12 July 1917 the *Irish Independent* prophetically warned that their attempts to win independence would merely bring 'dire misfortune and untold horrors, and ruin and devastation, and the demon of civil strife'.

There were close personal links and shared membership between Sinn Féin and the IRA; however, the IRB infiltration of the IRA was more or less total and in reality it was never fully under the control of the Dáil, despite what De Valera may have claimed. Cathal Brugha may have become Minister of Defence in April 1919, but it was soon obvious that the real power behind the IRA was the 'Big Fellow', Michael Collins, who was a senior member of the IRB. In fact, the independence of the IRA from the Dáil was what sowed the seeds for civil war in 1922.

All that, however, was in the future and the rebels released from Frongoch and elsewhere in 1917 were faced with that classic question, 'if you were to do it again how would you do it differently?' When the Armistice effectively ended the First World War on 11 November 1918 the IRA realized that any hope of aid from Germany had passed. In many ways, German defeat was not such a great blow to the Republican movement; after all they had armed both Unionists and Nationalists and had singularly failed to support the IRA during the 1916 rebellion. Consequently, the IRA decided to bide its time, lend support to Sinn Féin and

concentrate on identifying other sources of weapons. The British were convinced that Sinn Féin was behind the 1916 rising and that the 'Shinners' were preparing to go again. In an attempt to pre-empt this action they arrested most of Sinn Féin's leadership as the result of a largely fictitious German plot in 1918. The crux of the alleged 'German Plot' was that Sinn Féin and the Germans were conspiring to start a second 'Easter Rising' in Ireland. The police and army failed to catch the IRA's key players, which allowed these militants to shape the Nationalist agenda. Between 1916 and the winter of 1918 the IRA concentrated on stealing much-needed arms and ammunition from the British, and teaching its members how to use them. This policy was driven by a serious lack of modern military weapons, and the IRA had to rely upon shotguns, hunting rifles and handguns commandeered from farmers and private households. These weapons were well suited to close-quarter assassinations, but neither conveyed the correct martial image nor were suitable for engaging in combat with the Crown's forces. The IRA knew that the numerous sparsely manned RIC barracks scattered across rural Ireland 'at some crossroads', according to the infamous David Neligan, presented them with a possible source of weapons, but it would be January 1920 before they felt confident enough to conduct a systematic campaign against them.

Of course, the end of the war meant that not only were there hundreds of thousands of British soldiers demobilizing but also there were literally millions of surplus firearms sluicing around the UK and the rest of Europe. Guns, however, cost money, and although it was expressly forbidden by the IRA some Volunteers carried out armed robberies to obtain funds for the cause, whilst Collins (Minister for Finance) organized a Republican loan that raised over £370,000 in Ireland alone. The Dáil insisted that the loan was purely voluntary, although

Michael Collins as Commander in Chief of the Irish National Army in 1922. (Courtesy of National Library of Ireland, Photographic Archive)

many Unionists subscribed, which raises the question of how much intimidation was used to solicit this money. Refusal to subscribe could be construed as treason and invite bloody consequences.

Efforts to raise money in the home of the Fenians – America – were not terribly successful. The US government was non-committal and appeared unwilling to upset their British allies. Ironically, the Irish community in mainland Britain seemed more willing to lend tangible support to the cause than their American cousins were, including carrying out attacks on the mainland. Despite the IRA's ambivalence to communism, De Valera even approached the fledgling Soviet Union for funds and military aid. This did nothing to improve his standing in America and simply served to reinforce an erroneous British perception that the Irish troubles were all a Bolshevik plot stirred up by foreign agent provocateurs.

De Valera reputedly said that all he had to do was look into his own heart to know what the Irish people wanted. Consequently it never crossed either his or the rest of the Sinn Féin leadership's minds that the landslide victory in of 1918 was anything less than a mandate to embark upon a war of independence against the British. Although their manifesto alluded to '... any means necessary ...' it did not mention the use of armed force, nor did it state any intention to plunge Ireland into violent chaos, and it is possibly stretching credibility a little to claim that the majority of Irishmen and women both endorsed and supported the IRA's campaign. The insurrection that began in 1919 certainly enjoyed more support than the 1916 rising, but it is impossible to judge accurately by how much.

Dying for Ireland

If it is difficult to identify exactly when the Anglo-Irish War began, there is little dispute that the final and most violent phase of it began in Soloheadbeg Quarry, outside Tipperary, on the morning of 21 January 1919. It was the same day that the 1st Dáil met in the Mansion House in Dublin, although the two events were utterly unrelated. So far the IRA's operations had resembled a crime wave rather than an act of war, and as a result the British had relegated its response to a police matter.

Soloheadbeg Quarry

Some hard-liners feared that the IRA would fall apart if it did not begin to act more aggressively. One such man, the Vice Brigadier of the IRA's South Tipperary Brigade, Seán Treacy, believed that if his men were able to forcibly take gelignite from an armed police escort it would boost their arsenal, prestige and confidence. It is difficult to know whether Treacy intended to kill the escort as well, although it is likely that the prospect did not disturb him. He planned to ambush a consignment of gelignite being moved from the military barracks in Tipperary town to Soloheadbeg Quarry on 16 January. Despite them laying-up in an ambush position for several hours, the consignment did not show up until five days later. Over those five days the ambush party had shrunk to nine men from the local South Tipperary Brigade – Seamus Robinson (Brigade OC), Treacy (Vice Brigadier), Dan Breen (Quartermaster), Seán Hogan, Tim Crowe, Patrick McCormack, Patrick O'Dwyer, Michael Ryan and Jack O'Meara. Two Royal Irish Constabulary (RIC) constables accompanied by two County Council employees (Edward Godfrey and Patrick Flynn) guarded the gelignite. Godfrey

was driving a cart containing 168lbs of gelignite whilst Flynn had 38 detonators in his pockets.

Masked and armed with a .22 automatic rifle, Treacy stepped into the path of the oncoming policemen and issued a challenge. As the constables fumbled with their rifles he shot them with a .22 automatic rifle. As they fell the remainder of his men opened fire, killing the two policemen. Both James McDonnell, a 57-year-old married father of five from Co. Mayo, and 36-year-old Patrick O'Connell from Co. Cork were Irish Catholics, who were apparently typical village bobbies who happened to be in the wrong place at the wrong time. It is perhaps symptomatic of the RIC ethos that despite being surprised and outnumbered they had attempted to resist what they probably believed to be an armed robbery rather than an act of revolutionary violence.

With the exceptions of McDonnell and O'Connell, all of the participants in Soloheadbeg were local men, so when Breen's mask slipped either Flynn or Godfrey recognized him, and by 29 January the Government was offering a reward of £1,000 – no mean sum in 1919. Soloheadbeg sent a clear message to the British that the IRA was willing and able to and kill His Majesty's forces to achieve its ends. This message was further reinforced when the IRA's newspaper, *An tÓglach* (*The Volunteer*), told its readers that it was their duty 'morally and legally' to kill soldiers and policemen. It was nothing less than a declaration of war by the IRA.

The IRA's decision to target the police was not universally welcomed and both the press and the Catholic Church condemned their actions and rather naïvely believed that the Dáil would not sanction such violence. De Valera, however, was less circumspect, and claimed in 1921 that the IRA in their capacity as the armed forces of the Irish Republic had operated with the Dáil's approval since 1919, and as President he accepted full responsibility for its actions. The IRA was, however, very sensitive about negative press and on 21 December 1919 Paddy Clancy led 20–30 men into the offices of the *Irish Independent* and smashed up its printing presses.

A dozen or so local Volunteers ambushing a small group of policemen in a quiet country lane seems to be typical of IRA operations. These were local men who often knew the policemen they were ambushing and, more significantly, were probably known by them as well. Some of these ambushes resembled highway robbery, with masked men holding up bicycling 'Peelers' in order to steal their weapons, whilst others degenerated into vicious close-quarter gun battles that the outnumbered policemen usually lost.

Throughout 1919 there were instances of the IRA shouting warnings before they opened fire, and of policemen giving up their service revolvers and Lee Enfield .303 rifles without a fight and being sent on their way. Sadly, as the struggle progressed these incidents became rarer as both sides became less inclined to act chivalrously. As the majority of policemen were Irish, Sinn Féin knew that they needed to undermine them and drive a wedge between the police and the public. They hoped to do this by portraying them as 'brave and trusting Irishmen' duped by the British 'to attain their ends', and in April 1919 they ordered a boycott of all policemen, their families and friends that was reinforced by an IRA boycott in June 1920 and ruthlessly enforced where possible. People were forbidden all contact with policemen. Shops were vandalized for selling goods to the police – Mary Crean of Frenchpark, Co. Roscommon, had three pig rings inserted in her buttock for supplying food to a policeman, and Michael McCarthy of Caheragh, Co. Cork, even had his hearse burnt in July 1920 for burying one. Girls also had their heads shaved for walking out with 'Peelers'.

The boycott was only effective in some areas, most notably the IRA strongholds of the south-west. Bizarrely, the unarmed Dublin Metropolitan Police (DMP) seemed to be excluded from the boycott, and suffered relatively few casualties throughout the Troubles with only nine men, six of whom were G-Men, being killed by the IRA. If Sinn Féin hoped that they could undermine the Castle's authority by attacking the police they overlooked the simple fact that they did not offer any alternatives, leaving married men with little choice but to stick with the police.

Some policemen helped the IRA, and the G-Men Neligan, Broy, Kavanagh, MacNamara, Mannix and RIC Sgt McElligott were especially useful to Michael Collins. Given that roughly 70 per cent of the 513 policemen killed were Irish there can be little doubt that they were singled out specifically by the IRA. Along with policemen, Irish civil servants, magistrates and even the Viceroy were potential targets. In all the IRA failed three times to kill Field Marshal Lord French but succeeded in killing Sir Henry Wilson in 1922.

Although the military presented the IRA with a harder target it managed to carry out several successful operations against them. In March 1919 the IRA raided the military aerodrome at Collinstown and got away with 75 rifles and around 4,000 rounds of ammunition. On 16 June it ambushed a joint RIC–Army patrol near Rathclarin, wounding a policeman and a soldier before the remaining three men gave up their weapons and were sent on their way.

Despite a limited involvement in supporting the police, the Troubles were very much a sideshow for the army in 1919, which was much more concerned with the issue of demobilization and overseas commitments. So much so that on 27 August 1919 the General Officer Commanding in Chief (GOCinC) in Ireland, Sir Frederick Shaw, informed the RIC Inspector General (IG), Brigadier General Sir Joseph Byrne, that the army would no longer be able to provide detachments to support police outposts. Ultimately, the army's intelligence network run by Lt Col Winter in Dublin and Tom Barry's foil, Major Percival of the Essex Regiment in Cork, were their most effective contribution.

The sack of Fermoy, 8 September 1919

A few weeks later, members of the local IRA battalion led by their Brigade OC Liam Lynch ambushed 18 men of the King's Shropshire Light Infantry (KSLI) on the way to church in Fermoy, Co. Cork. The attack was well planned but in the ensuing scuffle a soldier was killed, three were wounded and Lynch was accidentally injured by one of his own men. The attackers got away with 13 rifles in waiting motorcars. Although the Fermoy garrison reacted quickly, Lynch had planned his escape well. As the IRA getaway cars passed pre-designated spots logs were thrown across the road to prevent further pursuit.

The raid was fêted as a coup by the IRA because it was its first direct attack on the army. Collins had personally authorized the raid on the condition that there were no casualties – a difficult thing to guarantee under the circumstances. As a result Sinn Féin and the IRA were immediately banned in Co. Cork, which led de Valera in New York to state that, 'the English are seeking to goad the people into open rebellion in the field'. Considering that the Government's strategy had, to date, been completely reactive, the opposite was blatantly true and it was the IRA that was attempting to provoke an over-reaction from the Castle.

The subsequent inquest on 8 September did not help matters when it condemned the attack but failed to reach a verdict of murder, as the IRA had not intended to kill the unfortunate rifleman. For his comrades this was all semantics, and that night a mob of men from the Buffs (Royal East Kent Regiment), KSLI and Royal Flying Corps (RFC, now RAF) – probably the worse for drink – ran amok in the town smashing shop windows and those of the inquest jury's foreman as well. Republican propagandists

rather over-egged the pudding by branding this the 'sack of Fermoy', but significantly it heralded a new pattern of violence – the reprisal.

It would be another six months or so before reprisals became routine and 11 months before they became part of official government policy. Reprisals were counter-productive in the sense that they were a blunt instrument and often alienated otherwise sympathetic civilians. Usually these reprisals were little more than drunken soldiers or policemen venting their spleen against property, but as the conflict progressed the murder of Sinn Féin/IRA supporters became more common. There is no evidence that the chain of command sanctioned reprisals even if some officers privately condoned them, but by mid-1920 RIC reports constantly warned that discipline had declined to the point that reprisals were almost inevitable given the frustrations of trying to deal with an elusive enemy who increasingly attacked off-duty soldiers and policemen.

The day after the 'sack' of Fermoy, RIC Inspector General (IG) Byrne complained to the Irish under-secretary about the withdrawal of army support and ordered his men to abandon the more isolated rural police stations. In all the RIC abandoned 434 of its 1,299 barracks. Most of them were left not because they were indefensible, but because the men who lived in them were too isolated to protect. On 14 February 1920 the IRA under Ernie O'Malley and Eoin O'Duffy managed to capture the RIC barracks at Ballytrain, Co. Monaghan. By the summer of 1920 the IRA had successfully attacked and destroyed over 351 vacated police barracks along with 15 occupied ones.

Ballytrain boosted IRA morale, as although no policemen were killed it was the first successful attack on a manned RIC barracks. Usually the RIC managed to fend off such attacks with relative ease despite the fact that these buildings were not built for defence. When the North Kerry IRA led by Humphrey Murphy failed to take the RIC barracks in Brosna on 5 June 1920, Sgt

Coughlin and his 12 constables jeered at the fleeing Volunteers calling them 'rainbow chasers'. To add insult to injury a policeman had provided a soundtrack to the bloodless firefight on a melodeon!

On 17 June the occupants of the RIC barracks in Listowel, Co. Kerry, were told that they were being reassigned to rural stations to assist the army. Despite the best efforts of County Inspector Poer O'Shea, 14 of them refused to obey this instruction. On 19 June the Divisional Police Commissioner for Munster, Lt Col Gerard Smyth DSO MID, and the RIC IG, General Tudor, attempted to defuse the situation. What happened next is remembered as the Listowel mutiny, and has passed into Nationalist legend.

Listowel mutiny

The only version of events to survive is that of Constable Jeremiah Mee, the leader of the mutiny. His account was published in the underground Sinn Féin newspaper *Irish Bulletin*, which claimed that Smyth told them to shoot IRA suspects on sight. Mee was so outraged that he said to Smyth, 'By your accent I take it you are an Englishman. You forget you are addressing Irishmen.' He then took off his cap, belt and bayonet, and handed them to Smyth, saying, 'These too are English. Take them as a present from me, and to hell with you, you murderer.'

Ironically, Smyth was from Bainbridge, Co. Down and like many Irishman of his class spoke with an Anglo-Irish accent. He certainly advocated greater cooperation between the army and the police, and was concerned with creating better defences for RIC stations. It is also true that in Order No. 5, issued on 17 June 1920, he directed

RIGHT The funeral of RIC District Inspector James Brady in Glasnevin, Dublin 1920. (Courtesy of National Library of Ireland, Photographic Archive)

FOLLOWING PAGE An IRA volunteer runs for cover during the fighting around the Customs House, Dublin in 1921. (Courtesy of National Library of Ireland, Photographic Archive)

policemen to shoot armed IRA men who did not surrender 'when ordered to do so', in other words, when challenged, not as Mee claimed 'on sight'. In paragraph four of the order he also specifically forbade reprisals as 'they bring discredit on the police ... I will deal most severely with any officer or man concerned in them.' Hardly the instructions of a man advocating murder.

Whether it was true or not, Mee's testimony was a death sentence for the

one-armed District Commissioner Smyth who was killed a month later, on 17 July, by six IRA men in the smoking room of the Cork Country Club. The mutiny may have been as high-minded and nationalistic as Mee implied, but it is also possible that neither he nor his compatriots fancied the risky business of rural policing and preferred dismissal. It is a little suspicious that the only version of events appeared in a Republican paper; however, Mee may have needed to establish his Republican credentials in order to avoid the all too common fate of ex-policemen – the assassin's bullet.

Direct assaults on police barracks were a new phenomenon and despite the belief that the RIC was some kind of paramilitary gendarmerie it had little to no experience of defending a building. In an attempt to 'buy in' this experience, on 8 May 1920 the RIC began recruiting ex-army officers known as

The Customs House, Dublin, burning during the IRA's failed attack. (Courtesy of National Library of Ireland, Photographic Archive)

'Defence of Barracks Sergeants' who would be paid £7 per week. They were not supposed to interfere with daily policing and had no authority over the constables they worked with unless the station was under attack – in other words, their role was purely military.

In all, 33 men were recruited and RIC stations became better defended, with steel shutters over the windows and barbed wire around the grounds. It may have made the barracks safer but it also made them cramped and claustrophobic places to be. The IRA's response was to increase its attacks on off-duty policemen, and according to police records just over half of the policemen killed were shot whilst at home, walking out with girlfriends, drinking in the pub or, as in the cases of Sgts Gibbons and Gilmartin, whilst recovering from illness in hospital. A circular issued by the RIC Acting Deputy IG, T.J.

Smith, on 4 February 1920 warned of the dangers of moving about whilst off-duty, especially at night, and advised that those living at home be escorted by armed men. Married policemen and their families were especially at risk. Not only were they being boycotted but they were incredibly vulnerable when off-duty at home. Many were faced with the stark choice of moving their families to safer areas and living in barracks, or continually placing both themselves and their families at risk by trying to live normal family lives. It was a difficult decision to make, but despite the dangers the casualty rolls show that even at the height of the violence many policemen and army officers chose to live with their families or in rented accommodation rather than stay in barracks.

Attacking police barracks certainly boosted IRA morale, and on 25 May 1921 over 100 Volunteers forced their way into the Dublin Customs House, the HQ of the Local Government Board and the repository of a significant archive of government documentation. The IRA torched the building, destroying thousands of irreplaceable documents, but the police and army managed to surround the building before they could escape and killed five of them before taking a further 70 prisoner. Arguably the raid had been a spectacular failure and severely damaged the Dublin IRA.

War in the shadows

Despite these attacks, the real war was fought in the shadows between the British intelligence services, Special Branch, G Division DMP and the secretive IRA. G Division traditionally played a key role in suppressing Republican subversion, and although it had only 18 detectives, between them they ran an extensive network of informers. Collins knew that defeating the G-Men was crucial if the IRA were to win and commented that, 'even when the new spy stepped into the shoes of an old one, he could not step into the old one's knowledge'.

Fortunately for Collins there were some G-Men that were willing to collaborate with the rebels, and on 7 April 1919 G-Man Eamonn Broy smuggled Collins into the Division's central archive in Brunswick Street, Dublin. As a result Collins now knew who the G-Men were, where they lived and more importantly what they knew about the IRA. At first Collins tried to warn the G-Men off intelligence work, but failed, so he decided to have them killed. In all the IRA killed six G-Men, including its head Assistant Commissioner William Redmond before the Truce in 1921.

Collins' instrument of choice for special operations, 'the Squad', had officially formed by September 1919 and was answerable only to him. However the Squad's first 'job' was killing Detective Sgt Pat Smyth in Dublin on 30 July 1919, making him the first G-Man to die at the hands of Collins' men. The Castle was oblivious to the fact that at least four of its detectives were active IRA men and never worked out how Collins stayed one step ahead of them. Not only had Collins compromised the postal system, he also recruited at least one of the cipher clerks in the Castle, whilst RIC Sgt Gerry Maher supplied him with police codes.

Collins ran his network of agents from a string of Dublin safe houses and cycled openly around the city exploiting the fact that the British had no idea what he looked like. The British tried several times to find him but only one man, an ex-soldier from Newcastle West, Co. Limerick, by the name of John Byrnes (aka Jameson) came close. Despite meeting Collins several times, his cover was blown before he could complete his mission and Paddy Daly executed him in Dublin on 2 April 1920. According to Daly his last words were 'God Bless the King. I would love to die for him.'

In August 1920, the Government passed the Restoration of Order in Ireland Act (ROIA), giving the police and army draconian powers to crush the IRA. ROIA certainly made life difficult for Collins and his cohorts, but despite the pressure he maintained his intelligence network. Collins' greatest coup came on 21 November 1920, 12 days after the British Prime Minister Lloyd George had claimed to 'have murder by the throat', when Collins effectively emasculated British intelligence operations in Dublin by locating and killing 11 members of a crack undercover team known retrospectively in Republican circles as the 'Cairo gang'. For the loss of one of Collins' men – Frank Teeling – the IRA had blinded the British Secret Service in the capital.

Bloody Sunday

That afternoon, men from the RIC and ADRIC cordoned off Croke Park Gaelic football ground in order to search for IRA sympathizers. Tension was high and tempers fragile and within minutes of the RIC's arrival, 12 civilians – including a woman, a child and one of the footballers – were shot dead. The Auxiliaries, especially, were in an ugly mood and a party of them murdered

THE REAL STRIKERS

A contemporary image of the 1913 'Bloody Sunday', which was less than complimentary about the DMP's conduct. (Courtesy of Jim Herlihy)

two of Collins' most valued Dublin IRA men, Richard McKee and Peadar Clancy, along with an unconnected Gaelic-Leaguer called Clune, in the guardroom of Dublin Castle. By the next day the events of 21 November had already been dubbed 'Bloody Sunday'.

The Dáil was determined to substitute British justice with its own, and in June 1919 it established its own system of courts and Republican police. To promote this system it was vital to undermine the British system, and so magistrates and judges joined the police as IRA targets. Although the IRA did establish a prison system of sorts, minor crimes were punished with beatings or exile. Many were tried in absentia and their bodies found dumped and labelled, 'Spies beware – shot by the IRA' or words to that effect. Others simply disappeared without trace. Unlike the British system, there was no appeal system and few of those arraigned were ever acquitted.

Because the British did not view the IRA as soldiers, they were put on trial as criminals when they were captured. Perhaps the most famous and controversial IRA man to be executed was an 18-year-old medical student

by the name of Kevin Barry in November 1920. Barry may have been the first rebel to hang since the end of the war but he was not the first Irishman. That honour went to RIC Constable 75719 William Mitchell, a fellow Irishman, who was executed for murdering a shopkeeper. Barry's death made him both a Republican hero and the subject of a stirring rebel ballad. Despite what the ballad says, Barry was not hanged for being Irish but for taking part in the cold-blooded killing of three unarmed soldiers collecting their unit's daily bread ration. The rebel propaganda machine made much of Kevin Barry's tender age; however, the three dead soldiers – Pte Marshall (20), Pte Thomas Humphries (19) and Pte Harold Washington (15) – were not exactly elderly. There was no evidence that Barry actually shot any of them but he was captured at the scene of the killings with a loaded revolver. The quality of evidence against Barry would have convicted him in both a British and even a later Irish court as an accessory if nothing else. On the grounds that the British had executed Constable Mitchell they had little alternative but to condemn him to hang.

There can be little doubt that the British were fairly complacent in 1919, underestimating the threat posed by the latest rebels and losing a lot of ground to the Republic's initial onslaught. In 1920, the Castle decided to go on to the offensive and reinforce the police to quash the IRA. Much has been made of the fact that large numbers of policemen resigned in 1920 and 1921, a fact that many attribute to the boycott and assassination campaign. It is true that some policemen did resign because of the IRA, but 63 per cent of RIC men serving in 1919 were still in the force when it was disbanded in May 1922. In fact, about 3 per cent of the RIC left in 1921, which is only slightly less than the London Metropolitan Police who lost 3.1 per cent of its manpower in the same year. The highest resignation rate was amongst the

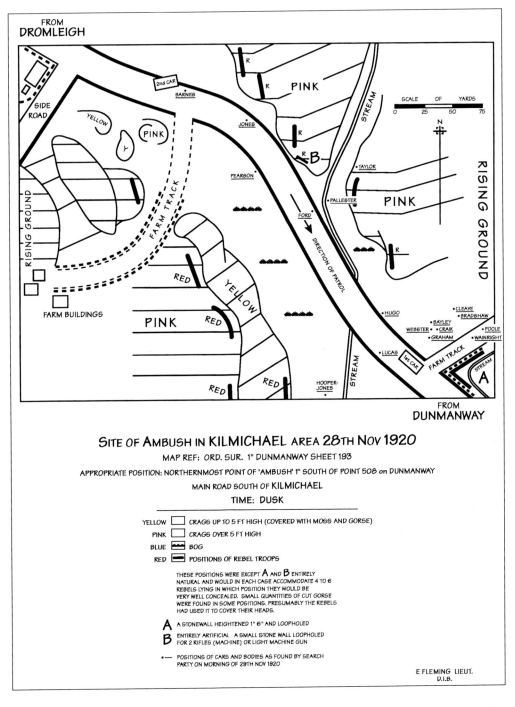

FROM
DROMLEIGH

SITE OF AMBUSH IN KILMICHAEL AREA 28TH NOV 1920

MAP REF: ORD. SUR. 1" DUNMANWAY SHEET 193

APPROPRIATE POSITION: NORTHERNMOST POINT OF 'AMBUSH' 1" SOUTH OF POINT 508 on DUNMANWAY

MAIN ROAD SOUTH OF **KILMICHAEL**

TIME: **DUSK**

YELLOW	☐	CRAGS UP TO 5 FT HIGH (COVERED WITH MOSS AND GORSE)
PINK	☐	CRAGS OVER 5 FT HIGH
BLUE	▰▰	BOG
RED	▰▰	POSITIONS OF REBEL TROOPS

THESE POSITIONS WERE EXCEPT **A** AND **B** ENTIRELY
NATURAL AND WOULD IN EACH CASE ACCOMMODATE 4 TO 6
REBELS LYING IN WHICH POSITION THEY WOULD BE
VERY WELL CONCEALED. SMALL QUANTITIES OF CUT GORSE
WERE FOUND IN SOME POSITIONS. PRESUMABLY THE REBELS
HAD USED IT TO COVER THEIR HEADS.

A A STONEWALL HEIGHTENED 1' 6" AND LOOPHOLED
B ENTIRELY ARTIFICIAL A SMALL STONE WALL LOOPHOLED
FOR 2 RIFLES (MACHINE) OR LIGHT MACHINE GUN

•— POSITIONS OF CARS AND BODIES AS FOUND BY SEARCH
PARTY ON MORNING OF 29TH NOV 1920

E FLEMING LIEUT.
D.I.B.

men recruited as Temporary Constables or Auxiliaries who, on the whole, had few emotional ties to Ireland.

The RIC began recruiting the men known to history as 'Black and Tans' in March 1920, to bolster the ranks of the police. It is true that there were tensions between the 'Tans' and the regular RIC, but they were not the monsters of legend. According to one IRA veteran some of the local IRA in Co. Mayo even agreed a ceasefire and drank with them on occasion until Collins sent some men to restart the war in the county. The big difference between the Tans and the rest of the RIC was that most of them were ex-soldiers who brought the mentality of the trench-raid to policing. The 2,200 men of the ADRIC or Auxiliaries brought another violent edge to the conflict. The ADRIC was meant to take the fight to the IRA and its men were based in the worst trouble spots.

Despite its reservations about ex-soldiers, the IRA did recruit them for their expertise. One of the most famous was the son of a policeman and ex-Royal Artillery Sergeant, Tom Barry, who helped train and then led the West Cork Brigade Flying Column. Barry was a ruthless guerrilla leader who prosecuted a merciless war against the Essex Regiment and the RIC.

On 28 November 1920, Barry ambushed two truckloads of Auxiliaries from C Company based in Macroom Castle. The ambush was an overwhelming success for the IRA, leaving 16 dead and one so badly injured that he was paraplegic for the rest of his life, for the cost of three dead Volunteers. One man, Cadet Guthrie, escaped but was later captured and murdered by the IRA who hid his body in a bog. As a result C Company was moved to Dublin and later disbanded.

The Kilmichael ambush, 28 November 1920

The IRA ambush that took place on the afternoon of Sunday 28 November 1920 on a quiet country road near Kilmichael, Co. Cork, is perhaps one of the best known and most controversial incidents of the Irish War of Independence. It is impossible to know exactly what actually happened, as several contradictory accounts survive. Even the man who commanded the IRA at Kilmichael, Tom Barry, produced different accounts of the event in his after-action report and in his memoirs.

Compared to the losses suffered by British forces in the First World War, or even Iraq in the 1920s, the British loss at Kilmichael of some 17 men was insignificant. However,

what was deeply significant was that members of the IRA's No. 3 (West) Cork Brigade managed to defeat an Auxiliary patrol in a conventional operation and undermine the Auxiliaries' reputation as 'super fighters'. The IRA commander, Tom Barry, carried out a classically simple and ruthlessly executed ambush employing cut-offs and killing groups to eliminate the police patrol.

Despite the fact that all of the policemen were combat veterans and many were decorated for bravery, they died at Kilmichael because they had become complacent, letting down their guard and failing to vary the routes used by their patrols. Barry claimed that he had known that the policemen would use the Kilmichael road as early as the Monday before, and that it was only a matter of time before he was able to spring his trap. In all probability, Barry did not intend any of the policemen to survive; after all, as an ex-British soldier he would have been aware that well-executed ambushes rarely leave survivors. It is more likely that Barry set out to kill all of the policemen in the patrol to send a message to both his own men and to the Auxiliaries. Barry was the son of a policeman and an ex-soldier and he needed to prove his Republican credentials to his IRA comrades-in-arms, whilst he also needed to break the psychological hold that the Auxiliaries had over many rebels by showing that they could be defeated. Nothing could more graphically serve that purpose than annihilating an ADRIC patrol.

The British later claimed that some of the policemen had been shot after they had surrendered, and that others had been mutilated with axes after they had been shot. There is, however, no evidence to support British claims that the bodies had been mutilated. In *Guerrilla Days*, Barry claimed that some of the British had pretended to surrender in order to lure his men into the open, and then fired on them killing Volunteers Michael McCarthy, Jim Sullivan and Pat Deasy and wounding Jack Hennesy, causing his men to ignore further pleas for mercy. What is perplexing is that

Locations of ADRIC companies

Company	Station	Town	County	Province
A	Woodstock House	Inistogue	Co. Kilkenny	Leinster
B		Templemore	Co. Tipperary	Munster
C	Macroom Castle	Macroom	Co. Cork	Munster
	Portobello Bks	Dublin	Co. Dublin	Leinster
D		Dublin	Co. Dublin	Leinster
E		Dublin	Co. Dublin	Leinster
F	Dublin Castle	Dublin	Co. Dublin	Leinster
G	Lakeside House	Killaloe	Co. Clare	Munster
H		Tralee	Co. Kerry	Munster
J	Macroom Castle	Macroom	Co. Cork	Munster
L	Mount Leader House	Millstreet	Co. Cork	Munster
M		Longford	Co. Longford	Leinster
O		Dunmanway	Co. Cork	Munster
Q	London and NW Railway Hotel	Dublin	Co. Dublin	Leinster
DEPOT	Curragh Camp	Curragh	Co. Kildare	Leinster

Barry did not mention the 'false surrender' in his report, nor do some of the other survivors of the attack. Another contradiction in Barry's *Guerrilla Days* is his claim that Cadet Cecil Guthrie was wounded and crawled off into a bog where he drowned. In reality he did escape the killing ground only to be captured and shot two days later by the IRA. It is hard to believe that one of the most active and effective IRA leaders in west Cork would have been unaware of Guthrie's fate or why he felt compelled to lie about it.

Although the truth will never be known as to what exactly happened at Kilmichael, there is a rough consensus over the course of events. Barry's scouts spotted the patrol, consisting of two lorries carrying men of No. 2 Section, C Company, ADRIC, at about 4.05pm coming from the direction of Macroom. Shortly afterwards the two vehicles entered the killing area and an IRA man dressed in full Volunteer Officers uniform, possibly Barry, stepped into the road and flagged them down. This ruse was intended to slow the lorries down so that they could be engaged with hand grenades. Whether the Auxiliaries mistook the man in the road for a British officer or not, the ruse worked and slowed the lead vehicle. The blast killed the driver and the passenger in the cab and a hail of gunfire quickly dealt with the remainder in the back. The map on p.55 clearly shows where each of the policemen died, indicating that, unlike those in the lead vehicle, the men in the second lorry had the chance to put up much more of a fight.

Cadet Guthrie, driving the second vehicle, attempted to manoeuvre out of danger but was prevented from doing so by one of the cut-off groups. A brisk firefight developed, and it was during this engagement that the 'false surrender' is said to have taken place. The

FOLLOWING PAGE British troops at the Jervis St Hospital, Dublin, after the Croke Park shootings in November 1920. (Courtesy of National Library of Ireland, Photographic Archive)

fight ended at close quarters and it is likely that British claims of post-mortem mutilation were in reality the bayonet and bullet wounds caused during hand-to-hand combat. In many respects Kilmichael was a typical ambush fought at short range, concluded in minutes and leaving no survivors.

In the lull that followed the storm, many of the IRA survivors were visibly shaken by what they had just done. Unlike Barry, most of them had never been in combat nor seen the detritus of battle before. In a move seen as callous by some, Barry berated his men for the loss of four men and then drilled them for five minutes amongst the British dead. According to Barry he did this to snap them out of their torpor by making them do something as familiar as drill. He was not alone in believing that routine mundane activity can help men cope with the trauma of combat. After removing the British weapons and the Auxiliaries' documents, Barry formed his men up and marched them away. By 11.00pm they were 11 miles away and spent the night in a cottage at Granure.

The IRA heralded Kilmichael as a great victory, and for the British it marked the single greatest loss of life in one incident. Barry's plan was extremely aggressive and his dispositions such that if his initial attack had failed to neutralize the British he would have had great difficulty in extracting his men. In short, he had created a situation where his men had no choice but to kill or be killed. Although the action was well executed and made Barry a rebel hero, it did little to change the course of the conflict and it would take another year of bloodshed before a negotiated settlement brought Irish independence.

Martial law and reprisals

The IRA did not enjoy support right across Ireland, and with the exception of metropolitan Dublin its heartland was Munster and parts of Connacht. As a result only eight of Ireland's 32 counties were ever placed under martial law. There was almost no IRA activity in Queen's County and

Leitrim, which would indicate that policing and everyday life changed little throughout the Troubles. Counties Meath, Kildare, Wexford and Wicklow were also relatively unaffected. In essence the struggle for Ireland focused around the Munster counties of Cork, Limerick, Kerry and Tipperary, where the bulk of army, police, IRA and civilian casualties were suffered. In the disturbed areas the British Army operated in conjunction with the RIC, and under ROIA IRA men could be tried by military courts rather than by civilian ones in order to prevent juries being intimidated. Military courts made it easier to convict IRA suspects and in the words of one newspaper report of 1920 in the *Morning Post* 'Whatever we may think of these reprisals in theory, in practice they are found to be the most effective way of causing murders to cease.' If anything they were counter-productive.

Other papers, such as the *Daily Mail*, agreed. When the army demolished several houses in Midleton, Co. Cork, on 1 January 1921: 'this is of course martial law. It is legal and disciplined. It is, we must believe, necessary. But it is horrible.' The reprisal was in response to an IRA ambush by members of the 4th Battalion, 1st Cork Brigade, when it killed three policemen and wounded five others on Midleton High Street on 29 December 1920.

Not all of the press was convinced about reprisals, and the *Galway Express* commented that 'when they throw petrol on a Sinn Feiner's house, they are merely pouring paraffin on the flames of Irish nationality'. *The Times* believed that 'the name of England is being sullied throughout the Empire ... however much they may seek to disclaim responsibility'. This paper was deeply uncomfortable with British soldiers and police using 'methods inexcusable even under the loose code of revolutionaries'.

An Auxiliary member of the RIC and a Black and Tan search an Irish civilian suspect. They were recruited by the British government to cope with the unrest in Ireland. Their reputation caused outcry in Britain and the USA. (Photo by Topical Press Agency/Getty Images)

'Tit-for-tat' warfare

Official reprisals were an attempt to control the anger and frustration of the thousands of policemen and soldiers who endured attacks by an elusive enemy. Much to the security forces' chagrin, on 28 September 1920 the RIC Deputy Inspector General C.A. Walsh issued a warning that anyone found taking the law into their own hands would be punished. In all, 766 policemen were dismissed for disciplinary offences and two, including the erstwhile Constable Mitchell, were executed for murder.

If military courts made convictions easier, the Government's habit of releasing convicted gunmen in its frequent amnesties created a frustrating 'revolving door'. This and the subsequent sense of betrayal was responsible for some policemen and soldiers creating anti-Sinn Féin societies that sent masked men – in all probability policemen – into rebel homes to murder Republican sympathizers in revenge for IRA killings. When the IRA killed Cadet Chapman at Dillon's Cross, Co. Cork, on 11 December 1920 an angry mob of policemen burnt down the city hall and most of St Patrick's Street in Cork, killing two suspected IRA men and wounding five civilians. Many Auxiliaries tactfully took to wearing half-burnt corks in their caps to 'celebrate' this act of retribution. Threats, however, were not enough for the men whose lives were now becoming dominated by the spectre of violence.

As the number of murders by 'Loyalists' increased, the IRA began to hit out at anyone they suspected of complicity. Irish Protestants increasingly became the targets of IRA murder and intimidation, as they were seen by many not as Irishmen of a different faith, but English settlers who were acting as a 'fifth column' for the Crown. In reality the Protestant community played little part in the Troubles in the South, much to the chagrin and disappointment of the Castle. The breakdown of law and order in parts of Ireland became an excuse for sectarian violence, and many Protestants died not because of their Unionism but because of the resentment of poorer Catholic neighbours.

Loyalist and Republican gunmen alike fuelled the bloody cycle of violence. When the IRA killed Constable Joseph Murtagh on 19 March 1920, masked men burst into Tomas MacCurtain's home at about 1.00am on 20 March 1920, and shot him dead. MacCurtain, the local IRA commander, was also the Lord Mayor of Cork. The lack of witnesses despite the proximity of a police station reinforced the widely held belief that the RIC had carried out the killing. In revenge, the IRA gunned down District Inspector Oswald Swanzy on 22 August 1920 as he left Christ Church Cathedral, Lisburn, on the orders of Collins who believed he had shot MacCurtain.

The IRA, however, did not enjoy much support in Loyalist Ulster, and Swanzy's murder sparked off rioting in Lisburn and Belfast that left 22 people dead and several houses burnt out. The rioting forced the authorities to enrol Special Constables on 24 August 1920. It was the first use of

Victims of IRA violence in mainland Britain, 1920–1922

K = killed W = wounded	Police		IRA		Civilians		Total	
	K	W	K	W	K	W	K	W
1920–July 1921	1	7	2	6	3	6	6	19
July 1921–1922	–	2	3	1	1	2	4	5
Total	1	9	5	7	4	8	10	24

Special Constables in the Troubles, and presaged the creation of the Ulster Special Constabulary or 'Specials' on 1 November 1920. Although the Chief of the Imperial General Staff, Sir Henry Wilson, disliked the fact that most Specials were in the UVF, in a similar vein to the adoption of 'official' reprisals, their use was probably the only chance that the Government had of controlling the forces that had been unleashed by the Troubles.

IRA operations in mainland Britain

The Troubles were not confined to Ireland but spilled over on to the mainland where IRA activists sought to bring the 'war' home to the British public. Over 1,000 men were on the IRA's books in Britain; however, only a couple of hundred at most were active. Between 1920 and July 1921 a total of six people were killed and 19 wounded in bombings and shootings whilst several thousand Irish men and women were detained for questioning and around 600 were formally arrested and charged. Collins, who had joined the Irish Republican Brotherhood (IRB) in London, never saw Britain as the main effort but viewed his people there as 'the auxiliaries of our attacking forces'. In reality, the IRA outside of London and Liverpool was relatively inactive although the Manchester battalion was responsible for 16 per cent of IRA activity in England.

In December 1920, Collins sent Paddy Daly to London to head up the IRA campaign. Until Daly's arrival mainland IRA units had little real idea of Collins' strategy and as a result missed several opportunities whilst awaiting orders. Between February and July 1921 they intensified their attacks on farms and factories in revenge for British reprisals against creameries and farms in Ireland. Explosives were rarely used, as arson was their main weapon, and despite the abundance of firearms they rarely seemed adequately prepared for direct confrontation with the police. The table on the previous page, taken from Peter Hart's book on the IRA at war between 1916 and 1923, illustrates the numbers of casualties suffered by both sides in mainland Britain.

In Liverpool and Tyneside, IRA men cut telephone and telegraph lines and there were several skirmishes between the police and the IRA in Merseyside. As in Ireland, the IRA was a police matter and even though the army played a supporting role, Special Branch and MI5 adopted a pre-emptive policy based on counter-espionage. The British were convinced that the IRA was a Bolshevik-inspired conspiracy, and gave the Government the excuse to extend DORA into a permanent Emergency Powers Act (1920), giving it extensive powers of arrest and detention.

On 4 May 1921 an IRA team shot dead two policemen whilst rescuing the commander of the Sligo Brigade from a prison van in Glasgow. Ten days later on 14 May they attacked 15 houses belonging to RIC Auxiliaries or their relatives, burning several out and killing one person. Compared to the bigger IRA organizations in Carlow, Westmeath and Waterford, the relatively small mainland IRA with 400–500 activists was much more aggressive. It burnt out 149 buildings and caused significant disruption to the Royal Mail, railways, roads and communication system at a cost to the British taxpayer of over £1.5m. The cost to the IRA was five dead, seven wounded and hundreds arrested.

The IRA had a vague idea that attacks on the mainland would focus attention on the Irish Troubles and undermine the morale of the British public, thus putting pressure on the Government. Although Ireland did feature regularly in the news and took up a significant amount of police effort, the campaign played second fiddle to Britain's other post-war problems. Ultimately the mainland IRA was a microcosm of its parent organization, and reflected all its factions and divisions.

David Neligan

It is very difficult to know accurately what the experience was like for the ordinary foot soldiers that fought the Anglo-Irish War. However, some survivors did write down their experiences, and one of the most unusual set of memoirs is probably that of David Neligan.

Neligan's experience of the violence between 1919 and 1923 was unique, as during this period he served as a Volunteer, G-Man, IRA Intelligence Officer, British Secret Service agent, National Army Intelligence Officer and founder of the *Garda Siochána* Detective Branch. His book, *The Spy in the Castle*, is highly readable and it is difficult not to like Neligan. Although his narrative appears to be frank and starkly honest in places, it is worth remembering that it is a subjective account of his time as a G-Man and IRA informer.

Considering many of the men killed in his story were known to him personally or were work colleagues, Neligan usually dismisses their deaths in the surprisingly bland factual statement 'he was shot by the IRA' without any emotional exposition. There can be no doubt that Neligan was a ruthless man whose work for Michael Collins led directly to the deaths of several men, and whose conduct of intelligence operations in Kerry during the civil war earned him the hatred of the anti-Treaty IRA.

Neligan was born in 1899, in Templeglantine, Co. Limerick, and was the youngest of eight children. He grew up in a happy, middle-class Catholic household and his book paints a picture of a rural Ireland more interested in labour shortages and foot and mouth than the climactic battles on the Western Front. Interestingly, Neligan never indicates that he had any intention of enlisting in the army to fight. In fact, the First World War hardly features in his account at all.

Regardless of how honest or otherwise Neligan's revelations are, they give some interesting insights into the life of both ordinary policemen and IRA activists at the time. Although two of Neligan's uncles were policemen and so were several of his father's friends, he joined the National Volunteers sometime before the Redmond–MacNeill split, so must have been about 15 when he joined.

He never knew which side of the schism his unit was on, which was in his words 'following the usual Irish pattern'. His unit was poorly equipped and 'had no arms except wooden guns', which seems to have been typical of many Volunteer units. Even though he was a Volunteer, Neligan decided to join the police in 1918 and even got a glowing reference from his parish priest.

In 1915 the Government had passed the Emergency Provisions (Police) Act, which placed a moratorium on police recruiting in order to keep the army up to strength. Despite his Nationalist sympathies, Neligan seems to have had little difficulty in enrolling in the Dublin Metropolitan Police (DMP). From his account he could have just as easily joined the Royal Irish Constabulary (RIC) but being stuck at some 'strategically placed crossroads' with three or four other 'Peelers' just did not appeal to him, despite the pay being better than the DMP.

Neligan tells us that promotion 'in both forces was as a result of examinations and open to Irish Roman Catholics' but that 'the top brass was reserved for English or Irish Protestants and Freemasons'. There were some Catholic senior officers, like DMP Assistant Commissioner Fergus Quinn, but they were rare. In Neligan's estimation 'religious and racial discrimination were rife'. Overall he paints a sympathetic picture of the police, and despite Sinn Féin's calls for a boycott of the police Neligan tells us that in

1918 the public still had confidence in the police force and joining was seen as a good job with good prospects.

Neligan felt that the rebels missed a trick by killing policemen rather than trying to win them over. Resignation records show that most of those who resigned were single men with little service. Married men needed to look after their families, and if the IRA prevented them from getting jobs when they resigned then they had little alternative other than to stick it out in the police or face starvation. Worse still, even if they resigned there was no guarantee that the IRA would not murder them anyway.

Neligan paints an affectionate picture of the DMP as a force full of decent men doing a thankless task for very little money. Their strength was that they had an intimate knowledge of their 'patch' and stuck together to the extent that 'the police would lie like devils inside and outside court to save a comrade'. Such was the close-knit world that Neligan entered in 1918 and ultimately betrayed. He joined the DMP mostly because, like so many country boys, the lure of the city as 'an unknown entity' was too much for him to resist. When he got to Dublin he discovered that much of it was squalid and over-crowded and in his estimation the DMP Depot in Kevin Street was little better.

Neligan's training was fairly uneventful, but his book gives a fascinating insight into life in the DMP and some of its characters, such as the dapper but elderly Constable Denis 'Count' O'Connor who was reputably the best-dressed copper in Dublin. He also explained how the DMP was divided into six uniformed divisions, A to F, and the infamous G Division.

G Division was a cross between the CID and the Special Branch, and dealt with civil

A rare photograph of David Neligan. (Courtesy of Jim Herlihy)

as well as criminal investigations. It relied on 18 detectives to keep tabs on Dublin's political and criminal underworld. Its members were known as G-Men long before the name was popularized in American gangster films – they operated in plain clothes and unlike the rest of the DMP they were armed. They carried notoriously unreliable .38 automatics, and Neligan's went off in his pocket on one occasion. One thing that stands out in Neligan's account is that all of the G-Men were very snappy dressers.

After a brief period working out of College Street Police Station and as a clerk in the G-Division archives in Brunswick (now

Pearse) Street, Neligan volunteered to become a G-Man at the end of 1919 because he was 'heartily tired of uniform and beat duties'. Before the Troubles Neligan tells us that G Division was difficult to get into, but casualties had made it unpopular.

Whilst in uniform Neligan had been amongst the party who had found the body of DMP Detective Sergeant (DS) Daniel Hoey after Collins' Squad had shot him outside the Central Police Station in Brunswick Street on 13 September 1919. Neligan also knew another victim of the Squad, DMP DS John Barton, killed by Sean Tracey on 29 November 1919. He probably even knew DMP DS Patrick Smyth who was killed on 30 July 1919. Neligan is very matter of fact about these killings but there is no evidence to suggest that he was behind these deaths. The men who probably were guilty of these murders were three other G-Men: DS Eamonn 'Ned' Broy, Detective Constable (DC) James McNamara and DC Kavanagh, who had worked for Collins since at least 1917. In fact, Broy even smuggled Collins into the G Division archives in Brunswick Street where he was able to assess just how much the Castle knew about his organization. Between them these men were responsible not only for the deaths of a number of British intelligence agents but also for damaging the Castle's efforts to contain the IRA.

Even after joining G Division Neligan remained acquainted with several Sinn Féin activists, including De Valera's secretary Paddy Sheehan. How and why Neligan knew Sheehan is never explained, but he does mention that he recognized DS Hoey from a Sinn Féin meeting without explaining why he was there himself. His brother Maurice was a Trade Union activist, and along with Sheehan they convinced Neligan to resign from the police, which he did on 11 May 1920. Before Neligan resigned he did make an offer to Sheehan to work for the rebels, but Sheehan declined to accept. When Collins heard of this he was furious that the opportunity to turn another G-Man had been squandered, and not long after his

resignation Neligan was contacted by the IRA and eventually met Collins in Dublin. It was the beginning of an association that would only come to an end when the IRA shot Collins during the civil war. On Collins' instructions Neligan made his way back to the Castle and told his old boss, Detective Chief Inspector (DCI) Bruton, that the IRA had threatened to kill him. Neligan always felt that Bruton did not really believe him, but he was reassigned to G Division nonetheless.

Neligan proved to be a valuable asset and was soon passing Collins high-grade intelligence. It was Neligan who told Collins that an ex-RIC District Inspector and Resident Magistrate, Alan Bell, was investigating how the rebels were funding their operations. Neligan betrayed Bell's address, movements and security arrangements and within days he was dead.

By 1921, G Division had been rendered more or less ineffective against the IRA. Five G-Men, including Assistant Commissioner William Redmond, had been murdered and at least four were IRA activists. Both RIC Special Branch and the Secret Service knew that something was wrong with G Division and consequently placed little reliance upon it. According to Neligan the division's parlous state was simply a symptom of a 'demoralized state practically finished'. Despite his IRA activities no one suspected Neligan of 'working for the enemy', and much to Collins' delight he managed to join the Secret Service in May 1921.

Neligan was extremely complimentary about the Secret Service, whom he claimed 'sent some of their crack operators here. I must say they were brave men who carried their lives in their hands.' Despite obvious admiration and a degree of empathy for them he provided much of the information that led to the mass killing of British agents in Dublin on 21 November 1920, which is perhaps a comment in itself about their efficiency.

When the civil war broke out, Neligan became a colonel in military intelligence where he earned a fearsome reputation in Co.

Kerry. He was allegedly involved in the torture and execution of several anti-Treaty IRA men in February 1922. The Free State commander, Paddy Daly, said that, 'Nobody asked me to take kid gloves to Kerry and I didn't.'

After the civil war ended, Neligan returned to the DMP as a Chief Superintendent heading up its post-war G Division, and eventually became the head of the Garda Detective Branch. By the time he retired he was in receipt of a pension from the British Government for his time in the DMP and Secret Service, and from the Irish Government for his time in the Garda. When asked in later life if he would do any of it again his answer was an unequivocal no – 'revolution devours its own children'.

Civilian life during the Troubles

Like the millions of other people in post-First World War Europe who found themselves citizens of new ethnic-based states, millions of Irish men and women ended this period as citizens of a state that had simply not existed when they were born. The trauma of the war and the political violence that followed it inevitably had a considerable impact upon the lives of ordinary Irish people. The First World War left tens of thousands of Irish women dependent upon army allowances whilst their husbands were away fighting. In addition, the appalling casualties of Gallipoli, the Somme and four years of mass warfare left thousands of widows and orphans whose financial security was tied to the British State and their loss virtually ignored by the Irish one.

Just as it would be a sweeping exaggeration to say that every Irishman was a Nationalist who aspired to an independent Irish Republic, so it would be a gross oversimplification to portray all people, in all parts of the country, as being affected by the Troubles. In 1916 the Easter Rising had been played out almost exclusively on the streets of Dublin and, except in an emotional sense, had little effect upon the everyday lives of the Irish. In fact, the Rising had been deeply unpopular and many Irish people saw it as a betrayal whilst the country was at war.

The violence of 1919–23 was far more widespread than it had been in 1916, but even then it was still quite localized. The struggle between the IRA and the Crown's forces was played out predominantly in Munster and to a lesser extent in Dublin. In 1919, 1920 and 1922 there was virtually no IRA activity against the British in Co. Leitrim, and the only significant IRA act was the killing of 35-year-old RIC Constable Wilfred Jones whilst he was walking with his girlfriend near his barracks in Ballinamore on 15 April 1921. Queens County (now Co. Laois) was also quiet during 1919 and 1920 and again in 1922. The only significant

event was the IRA killing of 26-year-old RIC Constable William Vanston from Belfast on 2 February 1921 as he left his father's house in Maryborough (now Port Laois).

Of course, the tempo of violence in the south-western counties was far higher, as was the instance of reprisals. Not only did more soldiers, policemen and IRA members become casualties in counties Cork, Limerick, Tipperary and Kerry, but the numbers of civilians metaphorically caught in the crossfire was significantly higher as well. It is difficult to calculate exactly how many civilians were killed between 1919 and 1923, although estimates range from 300 up to as high as 1,000 or so. The historian Peter

Dublin was the scene of several clashes between the Irish Army and the IRA during the civil war. (Courtesy of National Library of Ireland, Photographic Archive)

Hart suggests that at least 198 civilians were killed and 189 wounded between 1919 and 1921 in Co. Cork alone.

At the centre of the struggle between the Castle and the rebel Dáil was the struggle for the hearts and minds of the Irish population, as each side vied to establish itself as the legitimate government of Ireland. The Castle had the distinct advantage of being the de facto, and arguably *de jure*, government in 1918, with a functioning legal system and an effective police service. To supplant this, the Dáil needed to dismantle the British system and replace it with its own. This was the logic behind the IRA attacks on policemen and police stations.

Although the rebels did attempt to create an alternative judicial system and a 'Republican' police force, they also managed to create a climate of lawlessness in some areas that simply allowed rebels and Loyalists alike to commit arson, theft and murder with little chance of apprehension. The general breakdown of law and order was most marked in Munster and especially in Co. Cork. In the affected counties the civil population had a hard choice to make. If they refused to recognize the Crown's authority they were likely to fall victim to Government reprisals. The police and army singled out Republican sympathizers and destroyed their homes and goods with impunity. Alternatively, if they refused to recognize the authority of the Dáil they were likely to receive a midnight visit from the IRA who would deal with them as traitors to the Republic. Such treatment ranged from being 'tarred and feathered' and subjected to public ridicule, to exile and even execution. It is impossible to estimate how many 'collaborators' the IRA killed, but the bodies of men and women were found dumped on country roads on most days. Despite their paranoia about informers, evidence for Co. Cork suggests that of the 122 people shot as spies by the IRA between 1919 and 1923, only 38 actually passed information to the British. That means that 84 of those killed were entirely innocent of having done anything except attracting the suspicion of

the IRA. Vagrants or 'tinkers' were also frequent victims, although few people missed them and many communities were glad to be rid of them. Statistically 27 per cent of those the IRA suspected of being informers were tramps. In reality they were only 14 per cent of the RIC's sources, yet they made up 67 per cent of the non-combatants murdered in Co. Cork. Protestants also fell victim to IRA violence. Twenty-five per cent of those suspected of passing information to the British were Protestants, but they made up 64 per cent of those killed for allegedly doing so.

In reality, the Protestant population, rather than being a Loyalist 'fifth column', proved to be a deep disappointment to the British. One vocal Cork Protestant Loyalist by the name of Tom Bradfield commented that he was 'not like the rest of them round here', indicating that most Munster Protestants were painfully aware of their vulnerability and were unwilling to put their heads above the parapet. The IRA killed Bradfield for his vocal Unionism. Some tried to weather the storm, others simply moved to safer ground in Ulster or mainland Britain.

Between 15 April and 8 June 1920 Arthur Griffith managed to establish shadow Republican Courts under Austin Stack and Volunteer Police in 21 of Ireland's 32 counties. Their influence was non-existent in Ulster and strongest where the IRA had managed to supplant the Castle's authority. The *Irish Bulletin* reported that rebel police had arrested 84 people in the first two weeks of June 1920.

Of course, punishment was always an issue and investigative procedures were questionable at times. There is one recorded occasion when the RIC attempted to rescue men imprisoned by the IRA on an island off the west coast, but they refused to be rescued. Legend has it that their refusal was because they were loyal citizens of the Republic, although it is equally likely that they were afraid of what the IRA would do to them if they accepted help from the British.

Several county councils actually declared openly for the Republic and withheld funds that were intended for the Castle administration. This was a two-way street, and the Castle withheld central government funds intended for these areas. Ultimately this created the bizarre phenomenon of two alternative judicial and policing systems jockeying for position with each one attempting to undermine the power of the other, causing confusion, uncertainty and chaos.

Despite its obvious limitations, the Sinn Féin legal system did attempt to conduct its affairs in a recognizable and responsible fashion. As the British legal system broke down, people increasingly turned to the Republican courts for want of an alternative. For the civilians caught in the middle it must have been an awful situation. Unemployment in post-war Ireland was high, with ex-soldiers being amongst the worst affected. During the war the British had banned emigration in the hope that Ireland's young men would enlist, and after it was lifted Sinn Féin promptly banned it again, making any attempt to leave Ireland an offence punishable by the IRA.

Most traditional histories of the Troubles emphasize the transition of de facto authority from the Castle to the Dáil whilst ignoring the fact that in many places

Random searching of vehicles often did little more than disrupt traffic and alienate the public. (Courtesy of National Library of Ireland, Photographic Archive)

nothing much really changed. RIC Constable Patrick Larkin, a native of Oranmore, Co. Galway, accompanied by a group of Black and Tans, was once called out to deal with the unwarlike activity of cattle and horses wandering around on the roads outside Rathdrum, Co. Wicklow, in August 1920.

In normal times a man may have thought himself extremely fortunate to be able to afford a motorcar in the 1920s. During the Troubles, however, he was likely to have his vehicle commandeered by either the police or the IRA and if he was lucky he might see

it again in one piece. More often than not such vehicles were never seen again. The IRA dragged some men from their beds to dig trenches across the roads to disrupt superior mobility. By day the same men could find themselves being compelled by the RIC to fill in the same trenches to re-open the roads, and so it went on. Ultimately, most ordinary people tried to get on with their lives despite the upheaval all around them. This was, of course, made extremely difficult in some areas where the IRA and Crown forces were in competition for control. One activity that seems to have been utterly unaffected by the violence of 1916–23 was the 'sport of kings' – horse racing. General Macready, the General Officer Commanding

Not everyone was glad to see the British leave in 1922. (Courtesy of National Library of Ireland, Photographic Archive)

RIC Constable 70979 Patrick Joseph Larkin. (Courtesy of Jim Herlihy)

(GOC), had warned that if there was any trouble at race meetings or if any of his men were killed at them he would enforce a universal ban ending horse racing in Ireland. Horse racing was extremely popular amongst both sides in the struggle and the IRA realized that any action on their part to precipitate a ban would have serious consequences as far as popular support was concerned. As a result, racecourses became almost neutral ground where both rebels and Loyalists rubbed shoulders and offered the opportunity for some to discover whether they were on an IRA death list or not.

By 1922 the majority of the population in the United Kingdom and Ireland were tired of the seemingly endless hostilities, and in June the British offered a solution. They suggested that Nationalists should be granted a degree of independence in 26 of Ireland's 32 counties and that six of the nine counties of Ulster should form a state that would remain Protestant and part of the United Kingdom. The result of this June 1922 southern Irish General Election, or Partition Election as it is sometimes known, was a resounding 78 per cent in favour of the Treaty and, by implication, partition. This does not mean that the majority of ordinary Irish people wanted partition, but rather that most were so sick of the violence that they preferred any sort of peace to continued war. If partition did not come easily to Nationalist Ireland it would be wrong to see it as welcomed by the Unionists either. The Unionist leader Sir Edward Carson was a Dubliner by birth and would have preferred to see all of Ireland remain within the UK. As it was the Unionists cut their losses and settled for what they could.

Ulster may have been the heartland of Unionism but not all of its population was Protestant or Ulster-born. Because Belfast was the only industrial centre in an essentially agricultural country it drew Northern as well as Southern Catholics to it in much the same way as Glasgow and Liverpool. This helped swell the Catholic ghettos within the city, storing up potential problems for the future. Although Loyalist gunmen carried out sectarian killings in the North, not every Catholic who went to Belfast was a rebel at heart, and many moved there to gain both employment and sanctuary from the violence in the South.

The view from mainland Britain

The British public had some sympathy for Home Rule but there was very little public

Mr Ian MacPherson, Chief Secretary of State for Ireland
with Viscount French of Ypres and of High Lake in the
County of Roscommon, Lord Lieutenant of Ireland
(Courtesy of National Library of Ireland, Photographic
Archive)

support for the IRA's campaign of violence.
In fact, the Troubles 'over the water'
probably reinforced anti-Irish prejudice in
some quarters. Much of the British press was
uneasy with the methods employed by the
police and the army to suppress the rebels.
As early as 13 May 1918 the *Manchester
Guardian* reported that the appointment of
Lord French as Viceroy meant that 'the
government is preparing for some very evil
work in Ireland'. *The Times* was equally
critical: 'The name of England is being
sullied throughout the Empire and
throughout the World by this savagery
for which the government can no longer
escape, however much they may seek to
disclaim responsibility.'

Many in the British Government saw the
Troubles in Ireland as an irritating sideshow
in comparison to their other problems. The
army was heavily involved in suppressing a
bloody revolt in Iraq as well as trying to
cope with the demobilization of millions of
war-service soldiers. Sinn Féin was not alone
in increasing its vote in 1918; the Labour
party also gained support, whilst many
feared that Britain was on the verge of a
communist revolution. Ultimately there
was a war-weariness in 1919 that was absent
in 1914, which allowed the Irish rebels
to shove the country down the road to
independence. For Lloyd George the 'Irish
question' was threatened to destroy the
delicate balance of his Liberal–Conservative
coalition, and eventually it saw his
ultimate downfall and tore apart the Liberal
party. Once more England's adversity was
Ireland's opportunity.

Thomas Hornibrook

In 1891, 10 per cent of the population of the 26 counties that now constitute the Republic of Ireland was Protestant. By 1991 Protestants constituted a mere 3 per cent. Although this process of decline began in 1911, when the spectre of Home Rule began to rear its head, it had levelled off by 1926. It is not surprising that the most rapid period of decline was 1921–23, when the country was experiencing the most turmoil.

In many respects the Protestant population of Southern Ireland were the real losers in the Anglo-Irish War. For the most part they were Irish-born and their families had been in Ireland for hundreds of years, yet in the eyes of some Republicans, like the West Cork Republican activist Kathleen Keys McDonnell, they were 'foreigners'. To many Irish Catholics they were merely strangers in a strange land. One such alien in the land of his birth was Thomas Hornibrook of Ballygroman House, in the Bandon district of Co. Cork.

Overall Protestant population in 1891 was 10 per cent. In 1861 only Kilkenny had less than 6 per cent Protestants. Dublin had a Protestant population of 20 per cent, as did Monaghan and Cavan. In many respects, the Dunmanway area of Co. Cork was the Ulster of the south. Co. Cork's Protestant population numbered 8.3 per cent across the county, but was higher than the national average at 16 per cent in Dunmanway, and for several hundred years an uneasy coexistence existed between the Protestants and the Catholic majority. Unlike the Protestants in Ulster, most of Cork's were English by descent and Church of Ireland by faith rather than Scots Presbyterians. However, like their Ulster brethren there was a deeply ingrained fear of sectarian violence if law and order ever broke down, which engendered a siege mentality more usually associated with the Northern Protestants. In their cultural collective memory the massacres of 1641 and 1798 were as fresh in their minds as if they were in Ulster.

Thomas Hornibrook was a landowner who lived at Ballygroman, halfway between Bandon and Cork, and was typical of his caste. He served for at least ten years as a magistrate in Ballincollig and only resigned the bench under pressure from the IRA in 1921. He was a man of very strong Unionist convictions and, unlike most Cork Protestants, he was unafraid of voicing his support for the British governance of Ireland. He had a reputation for being a hard man, as did his son Sam.

Many Republicans viewed the Protestant community as a fifth column within their midst. Although there were plenty of Irish Catholics who worked for the Castle regime it was Ireland's Protestants who made up the bulk of the political and social elite. In many Nationalists' eyes it was the Protestant landlords, big business and Freemasons who kept the British regime operating in Ireland. Some Catholics did reach senior positions in the police, army and Civil Service but the perception was that the Castle positively discriminated in favour of the Protestants.

The Republicans had an especial dislike for Freemasons who they viewed as particularly pro-British. As a result, the IRA killed several Irishmen – like Tom Nagle and Francis Fitzmaurice, both from Dunmanway – who were Protestant Freemasons. This dislike was probably reinforced because policemen were barred from being members of any 'secret' societies except the Freemasons. It is strange that Republicans should have been so hostile towards the Freemasons when one considers that most of the founders of the United Irishmen, the spiritual ancestors of the IRA, were not only Protestants like Wolfe Tone, but also Freemasons themselves.

Troops hold back a crowd of civilians during a military round-up in Dublin. (Photo by Hulton Archive/Getty Images, © Hulton Archive/Stringer)

It is not known for certain that Hornibrook was a Mason, but it is extremely likely as both Nagle and Fitzmaurice were neighbours of his and members of the same Church of Ireland congregation. In the eyes of the rebels most landowners were Freemasons, and most landowners were pro-British, which meant that all Freemasons must be pro-British as well. By a similar train of logic all Freemasons were Protestant so all Protestants were Loyalists. This was most definitely not the case with James Buttimer of Dunmanway, who was a dedicated supporter of Home Rule. This did not stop the IRA from killing him in April 1922.

The West Cork IRA was convinced that the county's Protestants were behind the 'Protestant Action Group' that was responsible for the assassination of several Republicans. In reality, the Protestant Action Group was probably a front organization for a Loyalist death squad drawn from the ranks of the RIC or Auxiliaries. However, the Protestant community was a disappointment to the British security forces. James McDougall, a Scottish businessman in Cork, accused the county's Protestants of being 'spineless'. Tom Bradfield of Killowen, who was also killed by the IRA, was a rabid Unionist who proudly boasted that he was 'not like the rest of them around here'.

As the RIC was driven out of its more isolated stations in West Cork, and law and order began to break down, the Protestant community became fair game for robbers and land-grabbers. One Protestant, Joe Tanner, was forced out of his home by armed men who told him that 'as there is no law in the county now I will have to get back what belonged to my forefathers'. Despite being resident in Co. Cork for a few hundred years, men like Hornibrook, Tanner, Nagle and the rest were still outsiders. Many Cork Catholics referred to the Protestants as 'English' and one of the IRA men who attempted to assassinate Tom Bradfield's brother Henry is alleged to have boasted that they would 'soon have the English out of the county'.

As the Anglo-Irish War developed, Co. Cork experienced a crime wave. In 1918 there were only two armed robberies in Cork City, but by 1921 there had been over 41. The situation was much worse in the countryside. Tom Hornibrook was robbed several times of weapons and cattle. His robbers usually claimed to be commandeering his possessions 'in the name of the Republic', although most such seizures, especially those involving cattle, were simply old-fashioned theft.

As an ex-magistrate and well-to-do farmer, Hornibrook was a figure of envy for many of his Catholic neighbours, and several people claimed to be ex-tenants who had been evicted by Hornibrook and who deserved a share of his land. Evictions were always a very emotive issue and one that was bound to gain sympathy for evictees in Republican circles. We will never know what the outcome of this dispute was, as IRA gunmen killed Hornibrook and his son in April 1922 and his estate became property of the State.

On the night of 26 April 1922 a group of anti-Treaty IRA officers led by Michael O'Neill, the acting commander of the Bandon Battalion, broke into Ballygroman House. They had attempted to rouse the occupants but with no success and so had forced entry. O'Neill was shot in the chest by Hornibrook's son-in-law, Captain Herbert Woods. Charlie O'Donoghue, one of the IRA men, left by car for Bandon to get reinforcements. After a standoff lasting several hours Woods, along with Tom and Sam Hornibrook, agreed to surrender if their lives would be spared. Woods was beaten unconscious and all three were bundled into a car and driven into the south Cork hills. All three were tried by an impromptu IRA court martial and sentenced to death for the 'unlawful' killing of O'Neill. Woods was shot on the 26th and his body dragged behind a car for several miles in an act of revenge for the same thing being done to an IRA man, Walter Murphy, by British officers in 1921.

Tom and Sam Hornibrook were taken out

the next day and forced to dig their own graves. After he had finished digging, Tom Hornibrook tossed his shovel into the hole, turned to his assassins and apparently said, 'Go ahead.' Neither man's grave was ever found. Ballygroman House was burnt to the ground, the fences were torn down and no Irish newspapers reported the murders of Woods and the Hornibrooks. It was almost as if they had never existed.

Local Protestants were horrified, not at their killing by the IRA, but at their utter foolishness in trying to resist armed intruders in the middle of the night. At the inquest all of the blame for what happened on 26 and 27 April was firmly placed upon the shoulders of Woods and the Hornibrooks. Even though the IRA men never explained why they were there, nor even announced that they were IRA to the occupants of Ballygroman House, at O'Neill's inquest the conclusion was that he had been brutally murdered by Woods.

Charlie O'Donoghue later claimed that they had stopped at Ballygroman House because their car had run out of petrol, but that did not really explain why he was able to drive to Bandon for help after O'Neill was shot. It was likely that they had gone there to kill Hornibrook as O'Neill was convinced that he was involved in Loyalist paramilitary activity. In 1921 an IRA officer had informed another Cork Protestant, William Jagoe, that regardless of the Truce there were a number of Protestants who were going to be shot.

The incident at Ballygroman House sparked two further nights of violence as armed gangs raided Protestant households in the Dunmanway area, killing ten men. Both the Irish and British papers were outraged at the killings, and Sean Hales, a senior Cork IRA man, condemned the murders and promised to protect the Protestant community. By April 1922 Ireland was well on the way to civil war, and the Free State Government did not control Co. Cork. Several of the IRA who carried out the killings were heard to shout 'Take that you Orange Free Stater!' as they shot their victims. In the minds of the anti-Treaty IRA it was logical that if the Protestants had been Loyalists under the British then they would be pro-Treaty, and thus still their enemies. Sean Moylan, an anti-Treaty member of the Dáil and an IRA leader in north Cork, commented that 'if there is a war of extermination on us by God no Loyalist in North Cork will see its finish'.

Many Republicans were convinced that the Protestant community was working against them. British records, however, indicate that only a minority of Protestant civilians ever passed information to the security forces. During the civil war the number was even less. Because of Protestant attacks on Catholics in Northern Ireland Protestants in the South knew they were vulnerable and tried to keep their heads down. Their caution did not do them much good, however, as 64 per cent of those executed as spies by the IRA in Co. Cork were Protestants. Of the 122 people executed in Cork between 1919 and 1923, only 38 were actually British spies; most were executed because of what they represented rather than what they had actually done. Like the Hornibrooks, they did not 'fit in' in the 'New' Ireland and were effectively eliminated from it. Many more left for Northern Ireland or Britain to escape intimidation, which in the eyes of many rebels merely confirmed their guilt.

The Treaty divided the Republican movement. Many felt that Partition and retention of the Monarchy were a betrayal of the cause and soon it became apparent that the IRA was about to turn on itself. Initially the old rebel heartlands of Munster and parts of Dublin came out against the Treaty. When anti-Treaty rebels occupied the Four Courts the British made it clear that if the Free State Government did nothing about it they would. Using guns loaned to them by the British the National Army shelled the Four Courts and over the months that followed Free State troops equipped with British arms slowly regained control of the country.

From the start the anti-Treaty forces lacked a coherent plan and throughout the conflict surrendered the initiative to the Free State. The Free State forces also had an advantage that the British had always lacked: they knew who their enemies were. The fact that the majority of Irish voters had accepted the Treaty probably made the rebels' defeat inevitable, and as their numbers were whittled away by casualties and internment the tide inexorably turned against them. The death of the IRA Chief of Staff, Liam Lynch, at the hands of Free State troops was the final straw and the rebels dumped arms and melted back into society. The Free State Government had won on a technicality but the scars of the Civil War would take decades to heal.

A brief peace

The Truce

In order to try to end an increasingly squalid conflict, the British had attempted a constitutional settlement by passing the Government of Ireland Act (1920), which provided for two separate Irish parliaments: one in Belfast to govern Ulster and one in Dublin for the rest of Ireland, with the intention that they would eventually unite into one. Neither the rebels nor the Unionists were happy with this solution, which, like so many British attempts to solve Ireland's problems, was a fudge.

The king opened the Belfast Parliament on 22 June 1921 whilst its Dublin counterpart had a far less auspicious start. Only the four Unionist MPs for Trinity College and the 15 senators appointed by the Viceroy put in an appearance when it convened on 28 June. Facing the reality of the situation the Parliament adjourned indefinitely.

When De Valera returned from America on 23 December 1920 it was apparent to him that the IRA was not winning – but neither were the British. The British began to explore the possibility of coming to terms with the rebels, and in June began to ease off the pressure in order to facilitate the peace process. In spite of this, IRA violence escalated and British casualties rose as a result from roughly 30 casualties per week in March to 67 in the first week of June 1921. The army continued to hit back but in military terms neither side had the upper hand. Demoralized and frustrated, General Macready and the Southern Unionist leader the Earl of Middleton secretly met with Dáil representatives and agreed an informal ceasefire on 8 July 1921. When the Anglo-Irish Truce came into force on 11 July 1921 the war was effectively over. Both sides claimed victory, although the British were finding it extremely difficult to sustain operations, whilst in 1922 the then Chief of Staff of the IRA, Richard Mulcahy, told the Dáil that the IRA had been beaten.

Between the Easter Rising and the Truce over 2,000 people had lost their lives. Of the 3,000–5,000 active IRA men who took part in the struggle approximately 650 were killed and several thousand arrested. The British had approximately 66,000 troops and policemen of whom around 555 had been killed whilst 1,027 had also been wounded. In addition, at least 300 civilians had been murdered or simply vanished.

How the conflict ended

The most obvious consequence of the political violence between 1913 and 1923 was the creation of an independent Irish state free from British control. However, it was not an end to what could be called British influence on the Irish police and army. Partition also created the two principal Irish political parties in Southern Ireland, with Fine Gael having its roots in the pro-Treaty government that won the conflict and Fianna Fáil developing from the wreckage of the anti-Treaty Republican movement that lost it.

Arguably, the two key issues enshrined in the Treaty that had precipitated the civil war were the nature of Ireland's relationship with Britain and that of Partition. The Saorstát that was created by the Treaty was to all intents and purposes still a satellite of the UK, with the king as the Head of State and a member of the Commonwealth. It also left the UK with naval bases at Berehaven, Queenstown (Cobh), Belfast Lough (in Northern Ireland) and Lough Swilly.

Partition was a pragmatic solution and its supporters knew it. Free State victory in the civil war guaranteed that Ireland would remain a divided island for the foreseeable future. Ulster Unionists never ceased to suspect that Britain would shed itself of all responsibility for Ulster at the first opportunity, and so the years that followed were dedicated to strengthening the viability of Northern Ireland. In 1914 the Unionist leader Sir Edward Carson had seen himself as an Irishman who was British; by 2004 few Ulstermen would feel comfortable with the epithet 'Irish', preferring to call themselves 'Northern Irish' or simply British.

De Valera finally returned to power in 1932 and eventually Ireland became a Republic in 1948. Without a shot being fired and without the feared repercussions in the UK, Ireland had finally broken its political links with Britain. Under de Valera's leadership Ireland was the only Commonwealth country not to declare war in 1939 in order to emphasize its independence. Independent or not, over 34,000 Irish citizens volunteered to fight in the British armed forces.

Impact of the Anglo-Irish War

With hindsight the Truce turned out to be the end of direct confrontation between the nascent Irish State and Great Britain, but this was not so apparent at the time. In fact, the British ruthlessly played upon the possibility

British police and soldiers evacuate casualties after a shooting outside Liberty Hall, Dublin, 1921. (Courtesy of National Library of Ireland, Photographic Archive)

that the war could resume when they finally began to deal with the Dáil's representatives.

The Truce stripped the IRA of its anonymity and thus its principal weapon. Anonymity had allowed Collins to move

Lancia car and police post at the corner of May Street and Joy Street, Belfast, after the murder of Special Constables Thomas Cunningham and William Chermside in 1922. (Courtesy of the RUC George Cross Foundation)

freely around Dublin and his gunmen to melt into the crowd. When de Valera despatched Collins to London as one of the Irish negotiators his picture was splashed all over the British newspapers, rendering his principal defence useless.

There were also concerns about the level of fraternization that was beginning to develop between former adversaries in some areas. Even if the men on the ground were

pleased with the ceasefire, the leadership on both sides were well aware that the war could reignite if negotiations failed. In West Limerick the IRA leadership tried to instil a sense of imminent danger in their men, but fraternization continued.

Despite the Truce, low levels of violence continued in some areas and the IRA's centre of gravity shifted from Munster to Ulster. Ulster remained a sticking point in the negotiations and Collins had hoped that the IRA would be able to drive it back into the Nationalist fold. The treaty that was signed on 6 December 1921 excluded Ulster from its provisions and kept Ireland in the Commonwealth under the British Crown with the title of the Irish Free State. De Valera issued a statement objecting to the Treaty, but on 7 January 1922 the Dáil voted to accept the Treaty by 64 votes to 57. De

Valera and the other dissenters walked out of the Dáil on 10 January and the inexorable slide into civil war began. The subject of the six counties of Northern Ireland remained an emotive subject and was the main pitfall in Anglo-Irish relations until the signing of the Good Friday Agreement in 1998.

In the South the Protestant community was viewed with suspicion by many Nationalists, and although attacks on Protestants were never sanctioned by the Dáil or Irish Government policy, sectarian violence reduced the Protestant population of the 26-county Free State. Whether sanctioned by the Dáil or not, IRA men killed both rich and poor Protestants, driving them off their land and confiscating their property. The Protestant population of Co. Cork was particularly badly hit, and in April 1922 alone ten Protestants were murdered. The killers were never caught.

Those Protestants that remained in the independent Irish State suffered from a degree of discrimination that caused further emigration to the UK. When de Valera finally became President of the Irish Republic he told the Co. Clare Library Service that they should employ a Catholic Chief Librarian rather than a Protestant. Even Garrett FitzGerald, former Taoiseach and child of a mixed Protestant–Catholic marriage commented in his 1991 autobiography that 'if I were a Northern Protestant today, I cannot see how I could be attracted to getting involved with a state that is itself sectarian'.

Despite emotional ties to the concept of a united Ireland it is likely that by 1921 most Irishmen and women were happy to accept Partition if it meant an end to the almost interminable cycle of violence and murder. Collins felt that by signing the Treaty he was in fact signing his own death warrant, as he was well aware that some of his 'comrades' would be unable to accept Partition. He sold the Treaty as a stepping stone to future reunification on the grounds that the British would be unwilling and unable to cede Ulster at that time.

Northern Ireland after the Treaty

Although Collins was a signatory of the Anglo-Irish Treaty he did not fully abandon the hope that the remaining six counties of British Ulster could somehow be coerced into the Free State, as post-Treaty Ireland was now known. Even during the civil war, when Collins as Commander in Chief of the National Army was fighting to destroy the power of anti-Treaty IRA Irregulars in the Free State, he was plotting with them to overthrow British rule in the North.

The Boundary Commission set up as a result of the Treaty was also a bone of contention, and it was obvious that Lloyd George had allowed both Collins and Craig to infer totally different things from its terms of reference. Craig was determined to prevent the Commission from ceding any further territory to the Free State, whilst Collins was emphatic that large tracts of counties Fermanagh, Tyrone, Down, Derry and Armagh had been up for discussion. The Dáil had already surrendered the Ulster counties of Donegal, Monaghan and Cavan because of their Catholic majorities, and knew that any further sub-division of Ulster because of Catholic majorities in Fermanagh and Tyrone would render their new state untenable. Consequently, they resisted any attempts to undermine their position. This is not to say that representatives of Stormont and the Dáil did not communicate behind closed doors, but covert dialogue seemingly did not prevent Collins from ordering the assassination of Field Marshal Sir Henry Wilson, the ex-Chief of the Imperial General Staff and Unionist MP for North Down.

During the treaty negotiations Craig refused to countenance being part of a 'united' Irish delegation. Publicly the Unionists had no truck with the rebels whilst behind closed doors channels were kept open between the two groups. In many respects Lloyd George exploited his role as a 'go between' to manipulate both Collins and Craig. As a result both Collins and Craig had radically differing perceptions of the remit of the Border Commission and arguably the rebels only

Throughout 1921–22 the British Army handed their barracks over to the Free State's newly formed Irish National Army. (Courtesy of National Library of Ireland, Photographic Archive)

agreed to the Treaty because Lloyd George threatened an unprecedented escalation of the violence if peace talks broke down.

Sectarian violence was escalating and in March 1922 Craig invited Sir Henry Wilson to become his special advisor on security matters. Wilson, an Irish Protestant, was a rabid Unionist who had come to believe that force was useless against the rebels and that the use of the Ulster Volunteer Force (UVF) in the Ulster Special Constabulary (USC) was a grave mistake.

There is some confusion as to whether Collins actually ordered Wilson's assassination or not. Despite his willingness to order the deaths of policemen, soldiers and civil servants Collins was usually reluctant to order the assassination of high-profile British politicians. He did sanction three failed attempts on the Viceroy, Lord French, but in Wilson's case his killers may have been acting on their own initiative.

On 22 June 1922 two IRA men killed Wilson outside his house in London as he returned from unveiling a memorial to railwaymen who had died in the First World War. Ironically, both of his killers, Joseph O'Sullivan and Reginald Dunne, the second-in-command of the London IRA, were ex-soldiers. O'Sullivan had lost his leg at Ypres, which is why he was unable to run away after the shooting. Dunne refused to abandon his comrade and they were executed on Thursday 10 August 1922 at Wandsworth gaol.

Coming to terms with the past

A significant factor in the failure of most Irish rebellions was the lack of a major Continental threat to distract British attention from Ireland. There can be little doubt that the rebellion that culminated in Irish secession in 1921 was assisted by the tensions that preceded the outbreak of the First World War, the war itself and the chaos that followed it, creating the opportunity for militant Irish Nationalism to break its bonds with the British. As ever 'England's' adversity was Ireland's opportunity.

The 1916 rebellion had been an inconvenient distraction at a time when the UK was building up its forces for the Somme offensive of 1916. To many Irishmen it constituted a betrayal of trust whilst the UK was at war; to others it was the spark that lit the torch of liberation. Few can dispute that the army handled the aftermath badly, but it was ill prepared for counter-insurgency and justifiably distracted by greater matters in France and elsewhere.

After the First World War ended the army was torn between its colonial commitments and suppressing a violent and bloody rebellion in Iraq, whilst steadily trying to demob its war service personnel. British casualties in Iraq were far higher than they ever were in Ireland and for want of a coherent counter-insurgency doctrine the army did not really know how to cope with unrest within the UK. They also did not fully understand the problem they faced, and many senior politicians and soldiers were convinced that the Irish rebellion was actually the beginning of a Bolshevik coup in Britain.

It is, however, too simplistic to speak of the violence between 1913 and 1922 as an Irish 'war of independence' or liberation, because not all of the Irish wished to break the union with Britain. A significant number of Irishmen, both Protestant and Catholic, were content with the union and served in the civil administration, the police and the army in an attempt to preserve it. Ultimately, the Protestant heartland of Ulster was vehemently opposed to Home Rule or any weakening of Ireland's link to Britain and consequently made the struggle an internecine one.

The struggle for national self-determination may have united the broad spectrum of Irish Nationalist opinion but the withdrawal of British control from the 26 counties of Southern Ireland quickly cleaved them apart. Militant Republicans felt that the Treaty was a betrayal of everything that they had fought for and that an escalation, not cessation, of the conflict was the only acceptable course of action, whilst others were more realistic in their appreciation of the situation.

In many respects the 'civil war' in the South that followed the Treaty in 1922 was the physical manifestation of the divisions amongst Nationalists. Those who accepted the Treaty tended to be those who had favoured Home Rule rather than full-blown independence before the war, and were inclined towards a more democratic, consensus-based approach. On the other hand those who subscribed to a more dogmatic and doctrinaire Republicanism tended to reject the Treaty.

Defeat in the civil war did not destroy militant Republicanism, and its remnants smouldered for decades before flaring into life between 1956 and 1962 during the IRA border campaign, and again in 1969. The modern IRA has its roots in these times, posing a threat to both the Irish Free State and Northern Ireland.

Ironically, the National Army during the Irish Civil War quickly adopted attitudes towards the rebel IRA that were uncannily similar to those of the British a few months before. This was possibly because so many of the new army's officers and men had served in the British Army, or equally it may have been because they were faced with the harsh reality of trying to defeat an elusive guerrilla organization.

By 1923, the Free State's organs of state, its civil servants and many of its policemen and soldiers were basically the same men who had served in the Castle. From a military perspective the Anglo-Irish War taught the British Army and the Irish police much. By 1919 the Royal Irish Constabulary (RIC) had forgotten most of what it knew about counter-insurgency and the army had almost no Standing Operating Procedures for dealing with insurgents. The army had become adept at fighting battles, but despite Britain's extensive colonial possessions there was little expertise in anything else. All of its training had become focused on teaching its soldiers to conduct conventional operations on a massive scale.

The fact that the Crown's forces were conducting operations against people who were ostensibly 'British' and under the full glare of the media meant that methods that might have been tolerated in India or Africa were unacceptable in Ireland. Consequently, the army began to learn the art of waging low-intensity operations, and the Royal Ulster Constabulary (RUC) and Garda inherited a significant pool of expertise in counter-insurgency.

From a British perspective the Irish 'experience' proved invaluable in its later confrontations in Palestine, Cyprus and Malaya. It is easy to forget that some of the senior military officers who took part in these campaigns had served in Ireland between 1919 and 1922, and that several hundred ex-RIC men transferred to colonial constabularies.

Ireland's proximity to Britain made it inevitable that, despite the violence, the two countries would have to coexist. The fate of Ulster's Protestants aside, British concerns over Ireland were mainly about defence. The Treaty gave the UK control over several strategic facilities on the island and limited the size of the Irish Army. The British abandoned these facilities in 1938 just prior to the Second World War, perhaps because they believed that Ireland would enter the war along with the rest of the Commonwealth. Of course Ireland did not enter the war; however, her survival during the 'Emergency' was as dependent upon the North Atlantic convoys as the UK's. This policy of neutrality continued after 1949 when the Free State declared itself a Republic although its economic prosperity and strategic security were heavily intertwined with Britain's. The Republic's refusal to join NATO created problems for the Irish Defence Force, although it discovered a meaningful role in the 1960s when Ireland began to contribute to UN peacekeeping operations.

To many, the issue of Partition was a ticking bomb that would inevitably go off at some stage. The Protestant majority living in British Ulster feared that, despite Dublin's acceptance of the Treaty, they would renege on it at the first opportunity. As a result, the Stormont-based northern Government never fully accepted that the IRA was not being covertly sustained by the Irish State. This meant that the RUC had responsibilities for both conventional policing and internal security. The raising of the Ulster Special Constabulary (USC) from the Ulster Volunteer Force (UVF) did nothing to dispel Catholic suspicions that Ulster's institutions were inherently sectarian in nature. Again, this was a sweeping generalization as many Catholics remained loyal servants of the Crown and even rose to senior posts in the police, army and Northern Irish Civil Service. Arguably Nationalists were as guilty as Unionists of exploiting sectarian fears, anxieties and attitudes for their own gain.

After Partition, Northern Ireland was governed by its parliament in Stormont on the outskirts of Belfast. It was a microcosm of Westminster with a House of Lords and a House of Commons. Stormont was a devolved parliament very similar to the one that now sits in Edinburgh to govern Scotland. Its mandate dealt purely with the internal affairs of the Province. As a result, Ulster's internal affairs tended to be ignored by Westminster politicians until the breakdown of law and order in the late 1960s.

The Free State's legal status as a foreign country, albeit within the Commonwealth, meant that Northern Ireland had few direct dealings with it: that was the prerogative of the Foreign and Commonwealth Offices in Whitehall. Until both the Republic and the UK were members of the EU, the border was controlled and policed like any other international frontier. Much to the chagrin of the Northern authorities it was a porous border that enabled the IRA to infiltrate the Province almost with impunity. Despite northern concerns that the South did little to prevent it, the Garda and the Irish Army deployed significant resources to interdict IRA incursions.

Of course, not all IRA men were Southerners, and after 1969 the majority of its members were homegrown Ulstermen. However, Collins' opinion that the Treaty was not a final solution but the beginning of a process that would ultimately lead to a united independent Ireland left a suspicion in the Unionist psyche that under the right circumstances Britain would abandon Ulster. This probably has its roots in the fact that Partition had been intended as a temporary solution with reunification under the Crown as the ultimate goal. British policy towards Northern Ireland does not exclude the possibility of a re-united Ireland; however, it insists that it can only occur with the consent of its population.

The major legacy of the Troubles of 1913–22 is probably the proliferation of myths, half-truths and misinformation that grew out of them. In the words of the historian Oliver Knox, 'There is no such thing as Irish history at all – the past, the present and the future being the same thing, one and indistinguishable.' Irish history has regularly been distorted to serve contemporary political needs. Often what is remembered is not what happened, but what some wished to have happened. By

'internationalizing' the struggle, Nationalists have been able to portray the conflict as one between an overbearing colonial power and a conquered and subjugated nation.

The reality is that Ireland was an integrated part of the UK, and by the end of the 19th century the country was beginning to share in Britain's prosperity. It is true that there were awful slums in Dublin and poverty in the less-developed rural areas, but this was by no means a uniquely Irish phenomenon, as the same was true of most mainland cities and rural backwaters. Irishmen had held high rank in the army and political establishments. The Duke of Wellington, a Dubliner by birth, had even been Prime Minister. Admittedly, most had been Protestants. For Catholics it was not their 'Irishness' but their religion that was a hurdle to advancement. It should be noted that the same was true for English, Scots or Welsh Catholics until the mid-19th century.

Amongst Nationalists, the IRA of this period is remembered in equally black-and-white terms as a guerrilla army that took on the might of the British Empire and won. There is a tendency to draw a distinction between the 'old IRA' and its modern descendents that blurs a few of the realities of the conflict. Despite the claims of many a rebel song there were very few conventional engagements. The few that did occur, like Kilmichael, tended to be blown up in importance, distorting the overall picture. The IRA of the 1920s was just as capable of committing atrocities as that of the 1970s and Collins' Squad conducted an extremely effective assassination campaign.

In essence, the IRA's war was one against the police and the civil administration rather than against the army, and the number of soft targets attacked far outweighs the number of hard ones. A significant number of the 'British' who died were Irishmen who were at home with their families or out socializing when they were killed. In fact the 'Irishness' of the Crown's forces is the one major factor that has been all but edited out of most accounts of the Irish War of Independence. It was Irish soldiers who dealt with the initial stages of the 1916 rebellion, Irish policemen who attempted to enforce the King's Peace and Irish magistrates and judges who convicted IRA suspects. These men paid a heavy price and were singled out as traitors to their country, and in all over 50 per cent of the policemen and Crown servants killed were Irish by birth. Even many of the infamous Black and Tans and Auxiliaries were Irish. Far from being the scrapings of English gaols that ran away from serious trouble at every opportunity they were mostly war veterans whose military records were above average. Some were decorated for gallantry, most did not fully understand the nature of the conflict they found themselves involved in and few were adequately trained.

Despite the popular misconception, the Tans and the Auxiliary Division RIC (ADRIC) were not one and the same organization, but two separate bodies with different roles. The Tans were an integral part of the RIC, whilst the ADRIC supported the RIC and had a far more aggressive mission. Ultimately it was their inadequate training, the lack of a coherent doctrine and the brutalizing effect of their experiences in the First World War that led to ill discipline and violence. When policemen did commit atrocities it did nothing for Britain's cause; however, there is a tendency to forget that the rebels were equally capable of barbaric acts at times.

The greatest weakness perhaps was the British Government's lack of a coherent policy to settle the Irish problem. In attempting to balance the interests of the Unionists against those of the Nationalists the British managed to satisfy neither side. The British did not really understand the nature of the problem they faced and vacillated between viewing the rebellion as a crime wave and a Bolshevik agitation. In reality it was neither.

Sinn Féin's manifesto did not mention armed struggle, and it is unlikely that the majority of Irish people wanted the bloodshed that followed. Arguably its victory in the 1918 General Election was a protest vote rather than a mandate for civil war,

meant to fire a warning shot across Westminster's bows. The acceptance of the Treaty by the majority of the Southern electorate in 1922 possibly confirms this. With hindsight, if the British had handled the issue of Home Rule and the Easter Rising differently Ireland could have remained within the UK.

Reprisals, official or otherwise, did nothing to improve the situation and often drove otherwise neutral bystanders into the arms of the rebels. Whereas many could dismiss IRA atrocities as the actions of terrorists and criminals it was a different matter when the assassin or arsonist wore a British uniform. It would be wrong to say that the British Government condoned everything that was done in its name: it did not. Indeed, senior soldiers and policemen went to great lengths to try to prevent ill-discipline and criminal behaviour amongst their men. Its lack of coherent policy had simply unleashed forces it could not control.

The Dáil was equally guilty in that respect. De Valera claimed that the IRA acted as the armed forces of the Republic from as early as 1919; in reality it was never fully under the control of the civil authorities. In seeking to undermine each other's authority, both the Government and the rebels contributed to the lawlessness in parts of Ireland. Despite British policy failures, over 75 per cent of Ireland remained under civil rather than military control. Even where martial law was imposed, IRA suspects were subjected to a legal process before they were imprisoned, executed or released. The same cannot be said of some IRA men who were captured by the National Army during the civil war.

It is difficult to identify exactly when Ireland crossed the Rubicon on its road to war. The events surrounding Home Rule and the creation of the UVF and the National Volunteers in 1913 gave the first real indication that the country had begun the slippery descent into the abyss of internecine violence. In many ways the First World War was both a stay of execution and the last real opportunity to avert violence. In 1914 Nationalist Ireland answered the call to arms with as much enthusiasm as the Unionists. However, both traditions felt let down in 1918 for very different reasons.

In an age of limited communications Republicans ruthlessly exploited British mistakes to win over both Irish and American audiences. Although the executions that followed the Easter Rising were perfectly legal they damaged British standing and created a new crop of martyrs for the cause. In many respects it was this dimension of the conflict that was most significant and ultimately better handled by the rebels. Government atrocities were played up whilst IRA ones were ignored or justified in suitably martial terminology. The truth lies somewhere in the middle ground. The struggle for control of Ireland undermined the rule of law to such an extent that both sides carried out actions that were unworthy, and thus both sides share the blame. In fact, the wounds that were opened up during the Anglo-Irish War are only now beginning to heal. In July 2005, the IRA issued an historic statement declaring that it no longer condoned the use of violence in its efforts to achieve a united Ireland. The process of decommissioning will be a long, complicated and controversial one, but this statement alone marks the end of a war that began over 90 years earlier.

Despite ignoring its British past or blaming it for its historic ills, Southern Ireland is beginning to come to terms with its own history. More and more books are being published about the other Irish Divisions, the 10th and 16th, that fought with distinction at Gallipoli and on the Somme. There is even a degree of pride in some circles that the RIC and Dublin Metropolitan Police (DMP) were amongst the first modern police forces in the world, and that their influence can still be seen in both the Garda and the police service of Northern Ireland to this day.

The greatest tragedy, and perhaps one most ignored, was that whatever the name given to its phases, whether they be the Anglo-Irish War or the Irish Civil War that followed it, the protagonists on either side were mostly Irish. In the wider scheme of things the fact that the Irish and British are so closely intertwined politically, economically and more importantly by family ties, means that even if it is seen in simplistic 'Irish v. British' terms, the conflict was still a civil war. Arguably many rebels like Pearse, Childers, Connolly and Griffith had as much English, Scots or Welsh blood in their veins as many Unionists had Irish. In essence, the Troubles were an internal conflict between closely related peoples. That is perhaps why, as all civil wars inevitably are, the conflict was so bitter. It is the failure to grasp this fact that perpetuates so many of the misconceptions surrounding the Anglo-Irish War.

Further reading

Primary sources

Documents

Hansard, H. C. Deb. (series 5) vol. 82

PRO, Cabinet Office CAB 23/1/2 Extracts of War Cabinet Meetings

PRO Colonial Office, Inspector General and County Inspector's Monthly Confidential Reports, CO 904/102–16

PRO Colonial Office, RIC Weekly Summaries of Actions, CO 904/148–50

PRO Home Office, The 1916 Royal Commission on the Rebellion in Ireland, HO 45/10810/312350

PRO Home Office, 1919–20 Attempted Assassination of the Lord Lieutenant (Lord French), HO 45/10974/484819

PRO Home Office, 1916–18 Civilians Convicted by Field General Courts Martial. Treatment in English Prisons, HO 144/1453/311980

PRO Home Office, 1916–19 Internment of Irish Prisoners in UK, HO 144/1455/313106

PRO Home Office, RIC General Register of Service, HO 184 vols. 31–42, 15/7/1899 – 31/8/1922

PRO Home Office, RIC Officers' Register, HO 184 vols. 47–48, 19/3/1909 – 17/9/1921

PRO Home Office, RIC Auxiliary Division, HO 184 vols. 50–51, 23/7/1920 – 5/12/1921

PRO Parliamentary Papers, 1914, vol. 18

PRO War Office, Registered Files: Ireland, WO 32

PRO War Office, Judge Advocate General's Office: Courts Martial Proceedings. WO 71/344–359 (inclusive) Fields General Courts Martial against Civilians Accused of Armed Rebellion, 1916, WO 71

PRO War Office, Judge Advocate General's Office: Miscellaneous Records. Proclamations and Orders under Martial Law in Ireland 1916, 1917, 1920 and 1921, WO 93/16–29 inclusive WO 93

Publications

Coates, T. (2000) (ed.), *The Irish Uprising, Papers from the British Parliamentary Archive* (London: The Stationery Office)

Stephens, J. (1916 repr. 1978, 1992 & 2000), *The Insurrection in Dublin*, introduction by John A. Murphy (Gerrards Cross: Colin Smythe Ltd)

Sturgis, M. (1999), *The Last Days of Dublin Castle*, ed. Michael Hopkinson and Tim Pat Coogan (Dublin: Irish Academic Press)

Secondary sources

Articles

MacDonald, Z. (2001) 'Revisiting the Dark Figure', *British Journal of Criminology*, vol. 41 issue 1

Books

Abbott, R. (2000), *Police Casualties in Ireland 1919–1923* (Dublin: Mercier Press)

Adair, J. (1998), *Puritans: Religion and Politics in Seventeenth Century England and America* (Stroud: Sutton Publishing Ltd)

Allen, G. (1999), *The Garda Siochána* (London: Gill and MacMillan)

Babington, A. (1991), *Military Intervention in Britain: From the Gordon Riots to the Gibraltar Incident* (London & New York: Routledge)

Barry, T. (1995), *Guerrilla Days in Ireland* (New York: Robert Reinhart Publishers)

Bartlett, T., and Jeffrey, K. (1996) (eds.), *A Military History of Ireland* (Cambridge: Cambridge University Press)

Bell, P.M.H. (1998), *The Origins of the Second World War in Europe*, 2nd edn, 3rd imp. (London and New York: Longman)

Bennett, R. (1959; repr. 2000), *The Black and Tans* (Staplehurst: Spellmount Ltd)

Bowyer Bell, J. (1998), *The Dynamics of Armed Struggle* (London: Frank Cass Publishers)

Bowyer Bell, J. (1989), *The Secret Army: The IRA 1916–1979* (Dublin: Poolbeg Press Ltd)

Brady, C. (2000), *Guardians of the Peace* (Dublin: Prendeville Publishing)

Breen, D. (1964), *My Fight for Freedom* (London: Anvil Books)

Caputo, P. (1977), *A Rumour of War* (London: Macmillan)

Carr, W. (1990), *A History of Germany 1813–1990*, 4th edn (London: Edward Arnold)

Carver, Field Marshal Lord M. (1998), *Britain's Army in the 20th Century* (London: Macmillan)

Coppard, G. (1980), *With a Machinegun to Cambrai* (London: Papermac)

Coogan, T.P. (1993), *De Valera: Long Fellow, Long Shadow* (London: Arrow Books)

Coogan, T.P. (1971; repr. 1980, 1984 & 1987) *IRA* (London: Fontana Books)

Coogan, T.P. (1990) *Michael Collins* (London: Arrow Books)

Curtis, L. (1994), *The Cause of Ireland, from United Irishmen to Partition* (Belfast: Beyond the Pale Publications)

Doyle, R. (2000), *A Star Called Henry* (London: Vintage Books)

Emsley, C. (1996), *The English Police: A Political and Social History*, 2nd edn, 5th imp. (London & New York: Longman)

Emsley, C., and Weinberger, B. (1991) (eds.), *Policing Western Europe: Politics, Professionalism and Public Order, 1850–1940* (London: Greenwood Press)

Falls, C. (1996), *Elizabeth's Irish Wars* (London: Constable and Company Ltd)

Ferguson, N. (1999), *The Pity of War* (London: Penguin Books)

Foucault, M. (1991), *Discipline and Punishment: The Birth of Prison* (London: Penguin Books)

Hart, P. (1999), *The IRA and its Enemies, Violence and Community in Cork 1916–1923* (Oxford: Oxford University Press)

Hart, P. (2003), *The IRA at War 1916–23* (Oxford: Oxford University Press)

Haythornthwaite, P.J. (1994), *The World War One Source Book* (London: Arms and Armour Press)

Hazel, D. (1999), *Attrition* (Upavon: DETS(A))

Herlihy, J. (2001), *The Dublin Metropolitan Police: A Short History and Genealogical Guide* (Dublin: Four Courts Press)

Herlihy, J. (1999), *The Royal Irish Constabulary: A Complete Alphabetical List of Officers and Men, 1816–1922* (Dublin: Four Courts Press)

Herlihy, J. (1997), *The Royal Irish Constabulary: A Short History and Genealogical Guide* (Dublin: Four Courts Press)

Hezlet, Sir A. (1972), *The B Specials, A History of the Ulster Special Constabulary* (London: Tom Stacey Ltd)

Holmes, R. (1999), *The Western Front* (London: BBC Worldwide Ltd)

Hough, R. (1990), *Winston and Clementine, The Triumph of the Churchills* (London: Bantam Books)

Kautt, W., and Showalter, D. (1999), *The Anglo-Irish War* (London & New York: Praeger Publishing)

Kee, R. (1972), *The Green Flag, A History of Irish Nationalism* (London: Weidenfield and Nicolson)

Knox, O. (1997), *Rebels and Informers, Stirrings of Irish Independence* (London: John Murray)

Laffin, J. (1989), *Jackboot: The Story of the German Soldier* (London: Cassell & Company Ltd)

Lumsden, R. (1993), *The Allgemeine – SS* (London: Osprey Military)

Maguire, M., Morgan, R., and Reiner, R. (1997) (eds.), *The Oxford Handbook of Criminology*, 2nd edn (Oxford: Oxford University Press)

McLaughlin, E., and Muncie, J. (1996 repr. 1998) (eds.), *Controlling Crime* (London: Sage Publications & OU)

McNiffe, L. (1997), *A History of the Garda Siochána* (Dublin: Wolfhound Press)

M.I.5: The First Ten Years, 1909–1919 (London: Public Records Office, 1997)

Neillands, R. (1999), *The Great War Generals on the Western Front 1914–1918* (London: Robinson)

Neligan, D. (1968; repr. 1999), *The Spy in the Castle* (London: MacGibbon & Kee Ltd; repr. Dublin: Prendeville Publishing)

O'Connor, U. (1975), *The Troubles: The Struggle for Irish Freedom 1912–1922* (London: Mandarin Paperbacks)

O'Halpin, E. (1999), *Defending Ireland, The Irish State and its Enemies* (Oxford: Oxford University Press)

O'Sullivan, D.J. (1999), *Irish Constabularies 1822–1922* (Dublin: Mount Eagle Publications)

Pakenham, T. (1997), *The Year of Liberty, The Great Irish Rebellion of 1798,* 2nd edn (London: Abacus)

Phillips, K. (1999), *The Cousins' Wars: Religion, Politics and the Triumph of Anglo-America* (New York: Basic Books)

Reilly, T. (1999), *Cromwell: An Honourable Enemy* (Dingle: Brandon)

Reiner, R. (1985), *The Politics of the Police* (Hemel Hempstead: Harvester-Wheatsheaf)

Reith, C. (1952), *The Blind Eye of History* (London: Faber and Faber)

Ryder, C. (1989; repr. 1992, 1997 & 2000), *The RUC 1922–2000, A Force under Fire* (London: Arrow Books)

Sloan, G.R. (1997) *The Geopolitics of Anglo-Irish Relations in the Twentieth Century* (London: Leicester University Press)

Smith, M.L.R. (1995), *Fighting for Ireland? The Military Strategy of the Irish Republican Movement* (London and New York: Routledge)

Taylor, D. (1997), *The New Police in Nineteenth-Century England: Crime, Conflict and Control* (Manchester & New York: Manchester University Press)

Taylor, P. (1999), *Loyalists* (London: Bloomsbury)

Taylor, P. (1997) *Provos: The IRA and Sinn Féin* (London: Bloomsbury)

Thompson, E.P. (1991), *The Making of the English Working Class* (London: Penguin Books)

Thompson, F.M.L. (1990) (ed.), *Cambridge Social History*, vol. 3 (Cambridge: Cambridge University Press)

Townshend, C. (1998), *The British Campaign in Ireland, 1919–1921* (Oxford: Oxford University Press)

Townshend, C. (1999), *Ireland* (London: Edward Arnold)

Townshend, C. (1984), *Political Violence in Ireland* (Oxford: Oxford University Press)

Unpublished papers

Richard Abbot's papers on the RIC Auxiliary Division.

Index

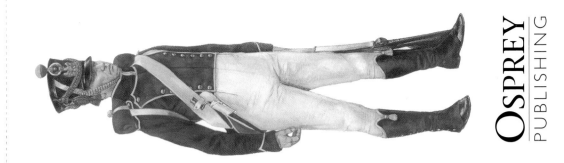

FIND OUT MORE ABOUT OSPREY

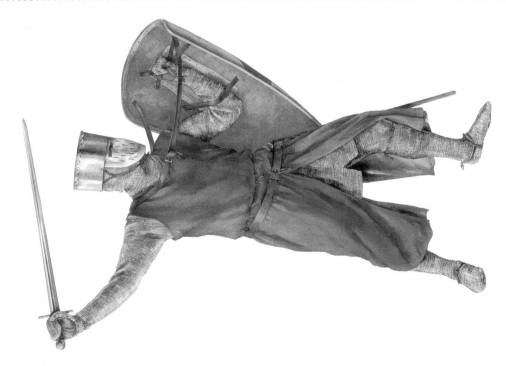

Young Guardsman
Figure taken from Warrior 22:
Imperial Guardsman 1799–1815
Published by Osprey
Illustrated by Richard Hook

www.ospreypublishing.com

OSPREY
PUBLISHING

Knight, c.1190
Figure taken from Warrior 1: *Norman Knight 950 – 1204 AD*
Published by Osprey
Illustrated by Christa Hook

POSTCARD